easy does it Quilts

Georgia Bonesteel

D1450321

Oxmoor House®

Contents

Easy-Does-It Quilts
From the *For the Love of Quilting* series
©1995 by Georgia Bonesteel

Published by Oxmoor House, Inc.,
and Leisure Arts, Inc.

Oxmoor House, Inc.
Book Division of Southern Progress Corporation
P.O. Box 2463, Birmingham, Alabama 35201

Library of Congress Catalog Card Number:
  95-68904
Hardcover ISBN: 0-8487-1480-6
Softcover ISBN: 0-8487-1468-7
Manufactured in the United States of America
First Printing 1995

Editor-in-Chief: Nancy J. Fitzpatrick
Senior Crafts Editor: Susan Ramey Cleveland
Senior Editor, Editorial Services: Olivia K. Wells
Art Director: James Boone

Easy-Does-It Quilts

Editor: Rhonda Richards Wamble
Editorial Assistant: Wendy L. Wolford
Copy Editor: Susan S. Cheatham
Copy Assistant: Jennifer K. Mathews
Designer: Eleanor Cameron
Senior Photographer: John O'Hagan
Photo Stylist: Katie Stoddard
Illustrator: Kelly Davis
Production and Distribution Director: Phillip Lee
Production Manager: Gail H. Morris
Associate Production Manager: Theresa L. Beste
Production Assistant: Marianne Jordan
Publishing Systems Administrator: Rick Tucker

A Day with Georgia

4

Ever wonder how this internationally known quilt designer spends a day in her own hometown of Hendersonville, North Carolina?

The Easy-Does-It Collection

6

Georgia uses her newest patchwork medley to show you how quilts can add warmth and zest to any room.

Georgia's Easy-Does-It Quiltmaking Basics

20

The First Lady of Quilts shares her wealth of quiltmaking tips and techniques.

Your Studio   20
Quilting Necessities   20
Rotary Roundup   22
Calculator Quilts   23
Easy-Does-It Piecing   23
Squares & Rectangles   24
Angle Aptitude   24
Easy-Does-It Appliqué   25
Borders   28
Quilting Primer   28
Binding the Quilt   31
Making a Hanging Sleeve   32

On the Cutting Edge

34

Georgia gives you template-free quiltmaking at its finest with these seven quilts and three pillows.

Rodeo Roundup 36
Baby Cowpoke 38
King-sized Cowpoke 41
Calico Crossover 42
Log Cabin Spin Wall Hanging 46
Quilt of Many Friends 50
Pillow Collection 54
Equilateral Love 58

A Novel Approach

100

Square yo-yo's and dimensional bow ties are just two of the novelty techniques that you'll find here.

Cuddle Quilts 102
Spinwheels 106
McAllister McPuff 108
Spooling Around 111
Antique Bow Tie 114
Bow Tie Doll Quilt 118
Recycled Tie Wearables 122

Contemporary Classics

62

"Traditional with a twist"—that's how Georgia describes the seven projects in this chapter.

Check & Double Check 64
Christmas Double Check
    Table Runner 70
Anvil & Stars 72
Fan Flowers 78
Cover Lovers' Cats 84
Brush Up 90
Diamond Flowers 94

Warming Up the World

126

Georgia travels all over the world collecting quilt inspirations. Here are some of the results.

Ukrainian Dolls 128
Ukrainian Dolls Wall Hanging 134
Yackety Yack 136
Tartan Thistle 140
Thistle Table Topper 146
Tartan Thistle Vest 147
Quilting Around the World 148
Tuxedo Friendship 152

Georgia's Gallery

158

In this picture gallery, Georgia shares her latest one-of-a-kind creations.

A day with Georgia

American Gothic in Hendersonville, North Carolina—my husband Pete and I pose in front of our Bonesteel Hardware and Quilt Corner.

Welcome to Hendersonville, North Carolina. Although quilting plays a major role in my life, it is not the only thing I enjoy. I like to do other activities every day, just to vary the routine. Come follow me through a typical day.

On a beautiful day, I enjoy cycling through historic downtown Hendersonville, my hometown.

Checking out the shops on Main Street, from flowers at the Curb Market to quilts at my favorite antiques shops, is always fun.

I always enjoy meeting fellow quilters in my travels and discussing new techniques with them.

My best thoughts come to me when I am walking. I make certain I always carry a pencil and pad of paper with me to record my ideas.

Tennis is a must each week.

My afternoon activities often consist of piecing, quilting, and, most importantly, playing with our cat Pee Wee. At the end of each day, I enjoy slowing down with a quiet evening of quilting.

5

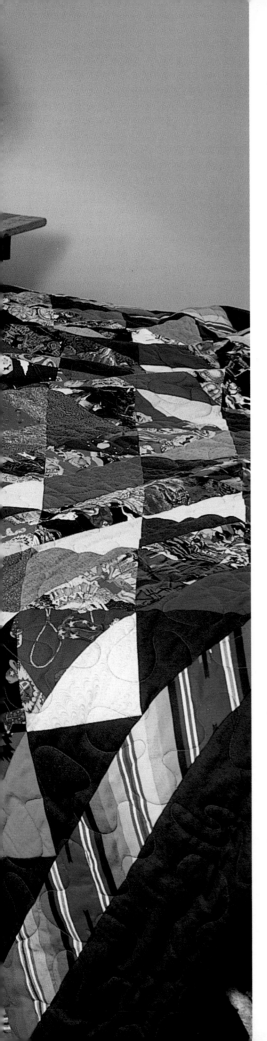

the easy-does-it collection

Quilts are no longer just for beds. When a room seems to lack a focal point, quilts can give it one. Let the following photographs inspire you to incorporate quilts throughout your house. You will find full-view photographs and instructions on the pages listed with each quilt.

KING-SIZED COWPOKE *(above)*
Large triangles show off a collection of just about every cowboy fabric ever printed. Made by Georgia J. Bonesteel. Instructions are on page 41.

BABY COWPOKE *(near left)*
Red bandana fabric frames triangles of navy and white for a great, cozy cover-up for cowboy dreams. Made by Georgia J. Bonesteel. Instructions begin on page 38.

RODEO ROUNDUP *(far left)*
Denim in every possible hue combines with an array of Western prints for this frontier-theme quilt. Made by Georgia J. Bonesteel. Instructions begin on page 36.

CALICO CROSSOVER *(above)*
Light and dark scraps combine to form an interlocking block design. Choose a handsome border print to pull it all together. Made by Georgia J. Bonesteel; quilted by Marie Detwiler. Instructions begin on page 42.

LOG CABIN SPIN WALL HANGING
(right) Update the traditional Log Cabin with vibrant colors and a snappy geometric design. Made by Barbara Swinea. Instructions begin on page 46.

PILLOW COLLECTION *(above)*
Bright fabrics in geometric arrangements lend a modern flair to these crisp settings. Left to right: Twirl, Indian Trail, and Spinoff. Made by Georgia J. Bonesteel. Instructions begin on page 54.

QUILT OF MANY FRIENDS *(left)*
Row after row of special signatures personalize this quilt. Made by the Western North Carolina Quilters Guild; assembled by Georgia J. Bonesteel; quilted by Nancy Cochran, the owner of the quilt. Instructions begin on page 50.

EQUILATERAL LOVE *(above)*
One equilateral triangle and a multitude of plaids produce an easy-does-it scrap quilt. Made by Georgia J. Bonesteel and Freedom Escape friends; quilted by Betty Nichols. Instructions begin on page 58.

ANVIL & STARS *(right)*
Use easy piecing techniques for traditional blocks as you make this striking quilt. Made by Keitha Kierbow. Instructions begin on page 72.

CHRISTMAS DOUBLE CHECK TABLE RUNNER (left)

Your table dressing is complete with this runner made in traditional holiday colors. Just one band from the Check & Double Check *quilt (below) does the trick! Made by Georgia J. Bonesteel. Instructions begin on page 70.*

CHECK & DOUBLE CHECK (below)

Reversible tartan plaids offset with bands of calico and light accents yield a quilt with Americana appeal. Made by Georgia J. Bonesteel; quilted by Shirley Henion. Instructions begin on page 64.

BRUSH UP *(right)*
Use the color wheel for inspiration as you select fabrics to paint your own artful quilt. Made by Georgia J. Bonesteel. Instructions begin on page 90.

McALLISTER McPUFF *(above)*
The yo-yo squares create a puffy "stuff-as-you-go" quilt. Made by Georgia J. Bonesteel and her mother, Virginia W. Jinkinson. Instructions begin on page 108.

COVER LOVERS' CATS *(right)*
Quilters and cats seem to have a natural affinity for one another. Make this cat quilt as a tribute to your furry friend. Adapted from a Betsy Freeman design; made by Georgia J. Bonesteel and the Cover Lovers quilt group. Instructions begin on page 84.

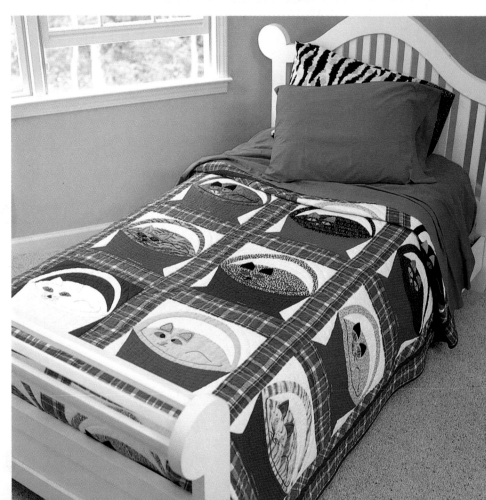

DIAMOND FLOWERS *(above)*
Delight in Log Cabin-style diamonds in this exquisite explosion of color. Inspired by the logo pin of the Bluebonnet Quilt Guild; designed by Georgia J. Bonesteel and Martine House; made by Martine House. Instructions begin on page 94.

FAN FLOWERS *(right)*
Traditional fan blocks become fan flowers in this vibrant appliqué quilt. Made by Georgia J. Bonesteel. Instructions begin on page 78.

CUDDLE QUILTS

They are cozy, they are quick—they are cuddle quilts! They are also samplers, combining a variety of featured techniques. A coordinated main print ties all the segments together. Instructions begin on page 102.

Made by Jo Ann Fuller.

Made by Alice Jarratt.

Made by Georgia J. Bonesteel.

Made by Conni Pelley.

ANTIQUE BOW TIE *(left)*
This quilt features a novel approach to the Bow Tie quilt—vertical bars of colorful ties. Made by Ingeborg Ness; from the collection of Irene Houg. Instructions begin on page 114.

BOW TIE DOLL QUILT *(below)*
This is the perfect little quilt for dolls and stuffed animals. This easy method has no set-in triangles. Made by Shirley Newman. Instructions begin on page 118.

SPINWHEELS *(above)*
Three-dimensional four-patch blocks twirl to create texture in this miniature quilt. Made by Shirley Newman. Instructions begin on page 106.

UKRAINIAN DOLLS WALL HANGING (left)

Search for the perfect border print and complementary fabrics to dress each figure. Made by Georgia J. Bonesteel. Instructions begin on page 134.

UKRAINIAN DOLLS (below)

Nesting matryoshka dolls add international flair to this colorful quilt. Designed by Georgia J. Bonesteel; made by Georgia J. Bonesteel and Middfest International Volunteers; quilted by Jan Becker and Georgia J. Bonesteel. Instructions begin on page 128.

TARTAN THISTLE *(right)*
A recent trip to Scotland visiting the tartan mills inspired the design for this colorful appliqué quilt. Made by Georgia J. Bonesteel. Instructions begin on page 140.

THISTLE TABLE TOPPER *(below)*
This easy-to-make table cover comes to life with two contrasting fabrics and frayed edges. Made by Georgia J. Bonesteel. Instructions are on page 146.

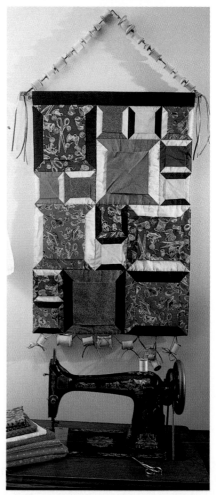

SPOOLING AROUND *(right)*
Decorate your special sewing space with—what else—spools! These spools are actually pockets that open up just enough to stuff with sewing necessities. Made by Georgia J. Bonesteel. Instructions begin on page 111.

YACKETY YACK *(left)*
Tessellated faces create positive and negative images. Made by Georgia J. Bonesteel. Instructions begin on page 136.

TUXEDO FRIENDSHIP *(above)*
Reminiscent of the Double Wedding Ring pattern, this quilt has oval rings made from feed sacks of long ago. Made by Penelope Wortman. Instructions begin on page 152.

QUILTING AROUND THE WORLD *(left)*
The love of quilting spans the globe. Accent your study with this tribute to quilting around the world. Made by Georgia J. Bonesteel. Instructions begin on page 148.

19

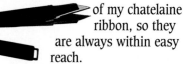

Georgia's **easy-does-it** QUILTMAKING BASICS

Quiltmaking offers you an opportunity to take bits of cloth and create your own unique piece of art. To make the most efficient use of this time, you should equip your workspace properly and learn the basics of patchwork. This chapter features those essentials.

Your Studio

It might be a large closet, a corner of the kitchen or the bedroom, or an entire room. Whenever I set up a make-believe studio for taping my Lap Quilting television shows, I'm amazed at how small an area one really needs to make a quilt. My workspace revolves around my sewing machine. I consider it an extension of my hands and my most important tool—and a very close friend.

From this focal point radiate the other three most valuable work stations: a cutting area; a place for an ironing board; and a viewing area. This viewing area can be a wall with a piece of cotton flannel or batting secured to its surface, or simply the floor space. Because I have a staircase in my studio, I just climb the stairs and look down onto the floor. Allowing space to make design and color decisions from a distance is important, since that is how we view the final product. You might also consider using a door peep hole (purchased at a hardware store) to create this distant view.

Quilting Necessities

Sewing Machine
The sewing machine is today's major tool for stitching patchwork, machine appliqué, and machine quilting. A machine with both straight and zigzag stitches works best.

Walking Foot
Useful for machine quilting, this sewing machine foot permits quilt layers to pass under the foot evenly. It is also useful when matching lines on plaid fabrics.

Scissors
Every quilter needs sharp scissors. My collection includes:

•*Thread clippers*—Thread clippers have a loop on top of the cap that allows me to secure them to the end of my chatelaine ribbon, so they are always within easy reach.

•*Thread nippers*—These are a must when cutting apart segments or trimming dog-ears at the machine. The round, single opening fits snugly onto the ring finger while the thumb and forefinger work the spring action.

•*Lightweight 8" shears*—Handy, lightweight shears make cutting a breeze, and they travel well, too.

•*All-purpose 8" scissors*—Sturdy, knife-edge, bent shears work well for heavy-duty cutting of multiple layers of fabric, as well as cutting silks, linens, or heavy wools.

•*Appliqué scissors*—These scissors feature an extended lip on one side of a 6" knife edge. They are made to grade seams and trim close to a stitched area.

Seam Ripper
This tool has a narrow blade designed to slip under threads to undo a mistake.

Stiletto

Instead of using your finger, try the stiletto for guiding seam allowances when sewing. Its long, extended pointer allows you to guide the fabric without the danger of getting your finger caught under the needle.

Pins and Pincushion

Quilter's pins have round heads for easy inserting and removing. The flat *flower pins* are great for rotary cutting, as the ruler will rest flat on top of the area where these pins are used.

Sewing Thread

For machine sewing, I use a cotton/polyester or a top-quality polyester thread. *For machine appliqué,* 100% cotton thread adds a sheen to the stitching. Match the top and bobbin thread when possible. Use an off-white thread for light fabrics and a dark gray or brown thread for dark fabrics.

Quilting Thread

Quilting thread *for hand quilting* comes in a variety of colors in both all-cotton and cotton/polyester blends. Some brands have a wax coating, which makes needle threading easier. *For machine quilting,* I use regular sewing thread with a coordinated bobbin thread. Monofilament thread comes in light and dark; use it as the top thread with a regular sewing thread in the bobbin.

Quilting Needles

Needles for hand quilting are called "betweens" and come in various sizes—the higher the number, the smaller the needle. I use sizes 10 and 12, but sizes 7 and 8 are good for beginners.

Thimbles

A thimble on the middle finger of the needle-holding hand is a necessity in quilting. I prefer a thimble with an indentation in the tip. This anchors the eye of the needle when I quilt. Sometimes I change thimble sizes during the day and even the season as my finger size varies.

Iron and Ironing Board

You will use both a dry iron and an iron on the steam setting in your quiltmaking. A small pressing mat is nice for workshops. Spray sizing (not spray starch) adds extra body to fabric that washing sometimes removes.

Pencils

Standard #2 pencils for marking grids and tracing onto fabric work well in quiltmaking.

Fabric Markers

For dark fabrics I use a chalk roller, thin soap slivers, or a white pencil. For light fabrics I use water-soluble pens (test on fabric first) or a pencil, very lightly. Be certain not to iron the water-soluble pen marks, and always remove all the markings with cool water once quilting is complete.

Pens

Never use a ball-point pen, as the ink can run and fade into a quilt—a lesson learned on one of my first quilts. Fine-point permanent markers are great for adding accent marks to appliqué, for signing and dating your quilts, and for tracing patterns onto template plastic or freezer paper.

Yardstick

A yardstick is a necessity in any sewing room. Mark its length into quarters and thirds to make a measuring stick you will refer to often.

Flexible Curve

This drafting tool has a metal, flexible core and a rubber outside that permits you to draw and sew curves for piecework and appliqué. It can also be used for altering patterns and for drawing curved quilting lines.

Template Material

Plastic, both plain and gridded, gives you a see-through surface for drafting geometric and free-form designs and appliqué shapes. Gridded freezer paper is an economical template material that adheres to fabric for cutting out shapes, permitting the grid of the paper to align with the fabric grain line. Bias edges are held firmly in place for cutting, and the paper provides a stable edge for stitching both patchwork and appliqué. Freezer-paper templates can be reused many times.

Stencils

Precut plastic quilting designs let you easily transfer quilting lines onto cloth. Build a small library of classic stencil designs, such as feathers, hearts, waves, etc., to use on your quilt projects. Border stencils usually have companion corner stencils to match.

Quilting Hoops and Frames

There are many kinds of hoops available. Wooden hoops come in round and oval shapes (14" to 22"), or you may prefer plastic lap frames in square or rectangular shapes. I prefer a 14" or 16" wooden hoop on a supported base. The quilt can rest on my lap so that my off arm does not have to hold the weight of a full quilt. Or you may prefer a long floor frame, which requires more space but allows friends to join you in quilting.

Quilt Clips

These plastic or metal bands hold the rolled layers of a quilt for machine quilting.

Color Wheel

A color wheel displays the full spectrum of colors—either on paper or fabric—and assists in color selection. It allows you to tell at a glance whether colors are complementary or contrasting.

Fabric

Good-quality, 100% cotton is the quilting fabric of choice for several reasons. It has good weight, it is strong, yet it is resilient and forgiving between seam intersections. Investing in quality fabric produces beautiful, long-lasting quilts. I prewash fabric with regular laundry detergent in the machine. Orvus paste also works well because it has a low pH factor and is gentle to the fabric. I eliminate any fabric that fades after continual washing.

Batting

Batting comes in cotton, polyester, polyester/cotton blends, and wool in a variety of thicknesses. Each brand carries instructions for care and handling. Certain quilts will lend themselves to a thin, flat look, while others require a thick, fluffy finish. Consider prewashed cotton flannel for batting in garments or in a thin summer quilt. Polar fleece works well as a combination batt-and-backing material, providing both texture and warmth (see *Cuddle Quilts,* page 102).

Rotary Roundup

Rotary cutters are available in many sizes and shapes. Find your favorite by testing them at your local fabric and quilt shops. I use two sizes: medium and small. The medium size is good for most projects and will cut four to six layers efficiently. I use the smaller cutter for miniature projects.

A self-healing mat is a necessary companion to the rotary cutter. Many sizes are available. For workshops and traveling, a small mat is nice; but for home, a 24" x 36" mat is my favorite. The ideal work station is a 35"-high cutting table with a full-size mat on the top. The precise 1" grid on the mat surface assists in aligning fabric.

Clear acrylic rulers complete your rotary-cutting equipment. Quite often these tools are available as a kit. Any quilting ruler should have accurate ⅛" and ¼" markings. The edges should be smooth and have legible markings that will not wear off. With so many sizes available today, it is hard to decide how many and which ones are best. I suggest you begin with the following:
- 6" square ruler
- 12½" square ruler
- 1" x 12½" narrow ruler
- 6" x 24" ruler
- 3" x 18" ruler

Rotary-Cutting Tips

- Learn how to change the blade in your rotary cutter.
- Always close the blade when not in use.
- Keep the blade pressed against the ruler and remember to press down on the fabric as you cut.
- Use the thick rulers, not the thin ones.
- Keep the bulk of the fabric to the right of the off hand (opposite for left-handed persons).
- Stagger folds of fabric so you do not start with a thick area.
- Store your extra blades in a plastic container.
- Let the outside fingers of the off hand fall off the ruler onto the mat to become an anchor between the ruler edge and the fabric or mat.
- Keep your rotary cutters in an old eyeglasses case, especially when traveling.
- Always stand when using your rotary cutter for better leverage.
- Don't lend your cutter to anyone—tell them I told you so!
- Cut away from yourself at all times.
- Your rotary tools make it easy to cut through several layers of fabric at a time. This way you can produce multiple shapes with a single cut.

Calculator Quilts

I depend on my calculator to figure yardage, to check border lengths, to determine quilt sizes, and to establish "quickie piece" segments to cut for stitching into blocks. Learning the decimal equivalent for eighths and quarters, plus the proper additions for seam allowances, lets me use my calculator to figure the cuts of half-square triangles and hexagons. I keep the following chart on a business card secured to the back of my calculator.

Fraction/Decimal Conversion Chart

$1/8$" = .125
$1/4$" = .25
$3/8$" = .375
$1/2$" = .5
$5/8$" = .625
$3/4$" = .75
$7/8$" = .875

Easy-Does-It Piecing

Remember, always use a $1/4$" seam allowance for patchwork. Some presser feet measure exactly $1/4$" from the right edge to the needle, providing a stitching guide. Be sure to test your own presser foot before piecing any pattern, as all math in this book is based on a $1/4$" seam allowance. If your presser foot edge allows for a larger seam allowance, you might consider purchasing a seam gauge for your machine or attaching a piece of masking tape to the throatplate as a guide.

Twirl Those Seams

Here's a great way to deal with bulky seam allowances when putting blocks together. This easy twirl leaves a soft intersection without a fabric-bulk problem on one side, and it allows the seam allowances to stagger automatically when they join.

1. Machine-stitch two sections together, with seams pressed in opposite directions *(Diagram 1)*.

2. Release seam allowance at the intersection only, using a seam ripper *(Diagram 2)*.

3. Twirl the joining seams in a circle—either clockwise or counterclockwise. The direction does not matter, but each block must twirl in the same direction for seam allowances to automatically stagger when they are sewn together *(Diagram 3)*. Press twirled seams open.

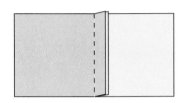
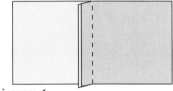

Diagram 1

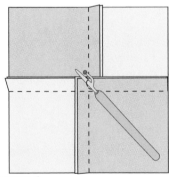

Diagram 2

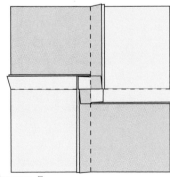

Diagram 3

Squares & Rectangles

You can create squares and rectangles with just two cuts. First, cut a strip from one or more layers of fabric the finished width of the finished square or rectangle plus ½" for seam allowances *(Diagram 4)*. To cut squares and rectangles from this strip, align the desired measurement on the ruler with the strip end and cut across the strip *(Diagram 5)*. Realign the ruler to make the next cut. Rely on the ruler measurements rather than the grid on the mat. *Log Cabin Spin* (page 47) uses repeated square and rectangle cuts.

Half-Square Triangles

Cut the square to be used to create half-square triangles ⅞" larger than the leg of the desired finished-size triangle. Cut the square in half diagonally to yield two half-square triangles *(Diagram 6)*. Trim the dog-ears that remain after you stitch and press a block made from half-square triangles *(Diagram 7)*.

Diagram 6

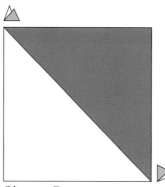

Diagram 7

Quarter-Square Triangles

Cut the square to be used to create quarter-square triangles 1¼" larger than the hypotenuse (long edge) of the desired finished-size triangle. Cut the square in quarters diagonally to yield four quarter-square triangles *(Diagram 8)*.

Diagram 8

Angle Aptitude

Bias Cuts

By using the 45° angle on your ruler, you can make true bias cuts. Place the 45° line on the selvage edge or the left top edge of a length of fabric and cut along the ruler edge to make a true bias edge *(Diagram 9)*. Then use this bias-cut edge as a guide to make further cuts of the desired width. *Check & Double Check* (page 65) uses the 45° angle for the plaid parallelograms. When cutting bias strips from the ties for the *Recycled Tie Wearables* (page 123), the 45° mark on the ruler is ideal for aligning with the stripes on the ties.

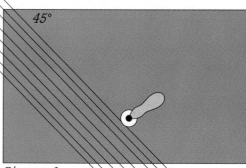

Diagram 9

60° Cuts and Equilateral Triangles

With the 60° angle on your ruler, you can cut angles that produce diamonds, as in *Diamond Flowers* (page 95). Determine the desired finished width of a diamond and add ½". Cut a strip of fabric to this width. Place the ruler on top of this strip, starting at the left end, and align the 60° angle with the top edge of the fabric. Cut along the ruler's edge. From this cut edge, measure the same width as above and cut a 60° diamond *(Diagram 10)*. Repeat to make additional diamonds.

For equilateral triangles, add ¾" to the desired finished height of the triangle. Cut strips of fabric to that width. For example, *Equilateral Love* (page 59) has finished triangles 5" high. I cut 5¾" strips and used the 60° angle on the ruler to make repeated cuts *(Diagram 11)*.

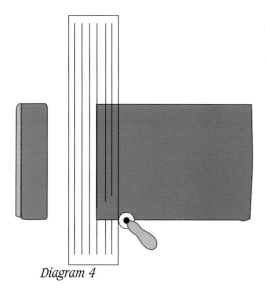

Diagram 4

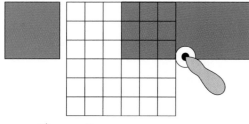

Diagram 5

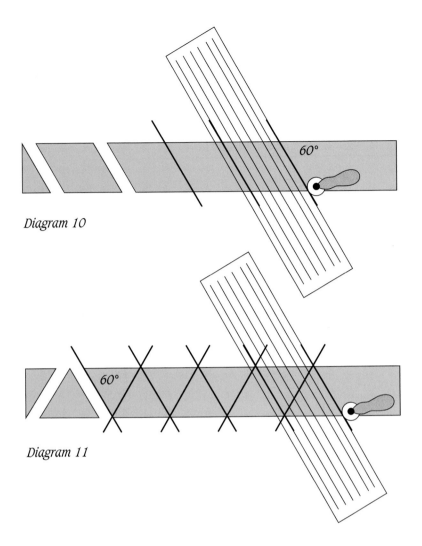

Diagram 10

Diagram 11

The Traditional Method

Lightly trace the finished-size appliqué shape onto the foundation as a guide. Turn under raw edges of the appliqué shape and baste, keeping the knot on the right side for easy removal later. Position the appliqué shape on the foundation and pin or tack it in place. Secure the edges with a small slipstitch, catching just the edge of the fold *(Diagram 14)*. Once complete, remove basting threads.

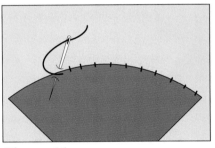

Diagram 14

Needle-turned Appliqué

Lightly trace the finished-size appliqué shape onto the foundation as a guide. Position the shape in place and baste, pin, or tack to secure. Finger-turn the raw edge under to begin, but then use the tip of the needle to turn under the edges as you stitch *(Diagram 15)*.

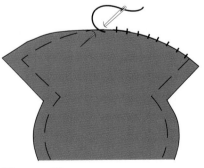

Diagram 15

Easy-Does-It Appliqué

To appliqué, you apply cut shapes to a fabric foundation either by hand or by machine. To make templates, trace the finished-size patterns from the book with a fine-tip permanent marker on template plastic or freezer paper. (For more information on using freezer paper for appliqué, see page 27.) Appliqué templates in this book are full-size with no seam allowances. Trace templates onto the fabric. *For hand appliqué,* add ¼" seam allowance when cutting out the shapes. *For machine appliqué,* cut out the shape directly on the drawn line.

Hand Appliqué

Cut shapes from fabric, adding ¼" seam allowance. Snip out tiny Vs on the seam allowance of convex (outward) curves so that the fullness will turn under easily *(Diagram 12)*. For concave (inward) curves, take tiny snips in the seam allowance, allowing it to expand *(Diagram 13)*.

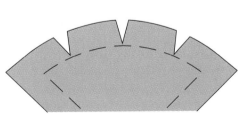

Diagram 12

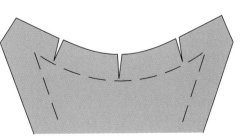

Diagram 13

Alternative Methods

After the ¼" seam allowance is turned under, you may secure the appliqué with a running stitch along the outside edge *(Diagram 16)*. Or you may choose the decorative buttonhole stitch, using a contrasting color of embroidery floss *(Diagram 17)*.

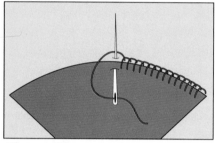

Diagram 16

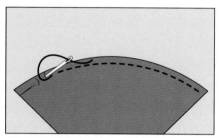

Diagram 17

Regardless of the method you use, you may want to trim away the foundation from the back once the appliqué is complete, especially if a light shape is appliquéd onto dark fabric. If so, be sure to leave a ¼" seam allowance as you trim.

Machine Appliqué

Cut shapes without a seam allowance. Secure the raw edges to the foundation with a satin stitch. Here are some tips to remember:

- Make a test sample first to determine thread choice, stitch width, and stitch length.
- Spray sizing (not starch) on the appliqué shape will add stability to the raw edges.
- Use a small amount of glue from a glue stick to hold the appliqué shape in place.
- Paper-backed fusible web can be used to secure appliqué shapes, but this adds an extra layer that may make quilting difficult.
- Place a paper stabilizer under the foundation to keep the satin stitch flat and even. Remove the paper once stitching is complete.
- Use the appropriate embroidery foot on your machine.
- When using the machine satin stitch, consider the needle position for outside turns. *For outside curves and corners,* stitch to the pivot point and stop with the needle down in the foundation fabric. Lift the presser foot, pivot the fabric, and continue stitching *(Diagram 18)*. *For inside curves and corners,* stop stitching at the pivot point with the needle down in the appliqué shape. Lift the presser foot, pivot, and continue stitching *(Diagram 19)*. *For sharp-angle corners* (as in the leaves on *Fan Flowers,* page 79), stitch down one side. As you approach a pointed end, start narrowing the width of the stitch *(Diagram 20)*. Pivot. As you stitch away from the pointed end, start widening the stitch again *(Diagram 21)*.

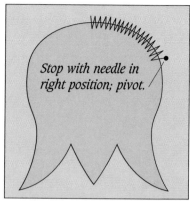

Stop with needle in right position; pivot.

Diagram 18

Stop and pivot.

Diagram 19

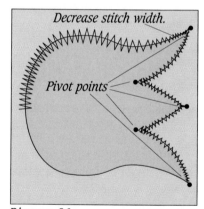

Decrease stitch width.

Pivot points

Diagram 20

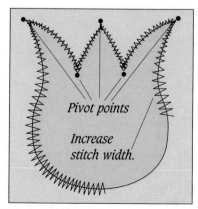

Pivot points

Increase stitch width.

Diagram 21

Five Ways to Use Freezer Paper for Appliqué

The ability of freezer paper to adhere to fabric has opened many new technique possibilities. Whether the coated side is placed facedown or faceup on the wrong side or the right side of the fabric depends on which of the following techniques you use. Adhere the paper with a dry iron on the cotton setting. Each freezer-paper shape can be reused many times before losing its ability to adhere to fabric.

Method 1

Press the paper template, coated side down, onto the wrong side of the fabric. Cut out the shape, adding ¼" seam allowance. Using the edge of the paper as a guide, needle-turn the seam allowance under as you stitch the shape to the foundation. Cut a slit in the foundation behind the appliqué and remove the paper. Or to reduce bulk, trim the foundation as described on page 26.

Method 2

Pin the paper template, coated side up, onto the wrong side of the fabric. Cut out the shape, adding ¼" seam allowance. Using only the tip of the iron, press the seam allowance over the edges of the paper *(Diagram 22)*.

Coated side of freezer paper

Diagram 22

Clip curves as needed to ease the fabric over the edge *(Diagram 23)*. Appliqué the shape onto the foundation. Cut a slit in the back of the foundation and remove the paper. Trim foundation fabric up to the seam allowance.

Coated side of freezer paper

Diagram 23

Method 3

Press the paper template, coated side down, onto the right side of the fabric. Cut out the shape, adding ¼" seam allowance. Pin the shape, paper side up, onto the foundation fabric. Appliqué in place, turning under the seam allowance up to the paper edge *(Diagram 24)*. Repress if the paper comes loose while stitching. Remove template when stitching is complete.

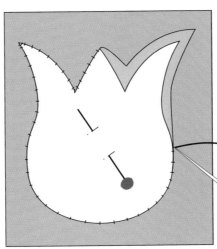

Diagram 24

Method 4

Press the paper template, coated side down, onto the right side of the fabric. Cut out the shape, adding ½" seam allowance. Place the shape, paper side up, onto the foundation. Using a paper stabilizer under the foundation, straightstitch close to the freezer paper. Use appliqué scissors to trim the excess appliqué fabric *(Diagram 25)*. Take care not to cut into the foundation. Remove the paper template. Satin-stitch over the raw edges, covering the previous line of stitching.

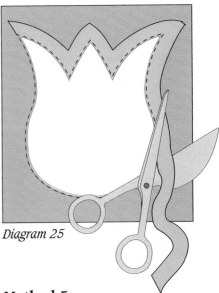

Diagram 25

Method 5

This variation of the previous method results in reverse machine appliqué. Press the paper template, coated side down, on the wrong side of the appliqué fabric. Cut out the shape, adding ½" seam allowance. Position the shape, paper side up, on the wrong side of the foundation. Pin. Straightstitch close to the freezer paper. Remove the paper template. Turn the work to the right side. Cut away the top fabric up to the line of stitching, revealing the fabric underneath. Place paper stabilizer underneath and satin-stitch over the raw edges. Remove the stabilizer and trim any excess fabric *(Tartan Thistle, page 141, uses this technique)*.

Borders

For each of the quilts and projects featured in *Easy-Does-It Quilts*, I have provided mathematically correct fabric amounts and dimensions for the borders. However, I suggest that you cut the borders after your blocks or sections are complete and sewn together. That way, if the size of your finished quilt top differs from that given in the book, you can still be sure that the borders will fit. Measure your quilt top on a flat surface, taking care not to stretch the sides. Measure through the length and width of the quilt instead of along the edges and add ½" for seam allowances. For a mitered border, add twice the width of the border plus ½" seam allowance. Join the borders to the quilt top, easing the quilt sides to fit the borders if necessary.

Most borders in this book are pieced to conserve fabric. I join border sections using a 45° angle. The fabric threads tend to blend together better than a straight 90° seam, and the seams can be placed anywhere. I find the following tips helpful in diagonal piecing:

• Cut strips the required width of the border. With right sides up, stack borders and cut a perfect 45° angle on one end of each segment *(Diagram 26)*. If the border requires three or more segments, both ends of the center segments must be cut at a 45° angle.

• To join border strips to each other, stack them with right sides facing and angled edges aligned. Stitch along the diagonal edge *(Diagram 27)*. Trim dog-ears after pressing. Then cut the border to the desired length.

Quilting Primer

After the quilt top is assembled, it's time to plan your quilting lines—the icing on the cake—to enhance your patchwork design.

To decide on a quilting pattern, first evaluate your block. Does it have direction? Do you want to emphasize star points? What is the overall feeling? The most traditional form of quilting is outline quilting, which emphasizes the piecework with the quilting lines stitched ⅛" or ¼" from the pieced seams *(Diagram 28)*. However, original quilting designs can set your quilt apart and make it truly your own.

A new quilting trend is to add quilting lines that contrast with the block design. For example, use a fan design on top of a Log Cabin square or a feather wreath with a star pattern *(Diagram 29)*.

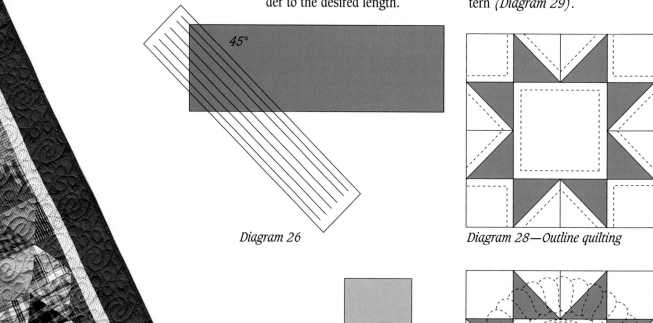

Diagram 26

Diagram 27

Diagram 28—Outline quilting

Diagram 29—Contrasting quilting

Transferring Stencils

The method of transferring quilting stencils varies, depending upon your supplies and preference. Pencils, soap slivers, water-soluble pens, or soapstone markers are all possibilities. If the stencil design is on paper, try using a light box or taping the stencil to a sunny window and placing the cloth on top for marking. A glass-topped table with a light underneath works equally well. Purchased precut stencils or stencils that you make yourself from plastic are both popular and durable. And since they are clear, you can see through to the fabric for easy placement.

Basting

Since you do not want your three layers—quilt top, batting, and backing—to shift while you are quilting, it is necessary to baste them together first. Basting is an important step, regardless of the manner in which you quilt. Insufficient basting will cause tucks and irregularities in the backing as you quilt. Align all corners and pin in place. Using a contrasting thread, take long basting stitches that you can easily remove later. Start basting in the center of the quilt and work outward.

The Foolproof Knot

Use the foolproof knot when you prefer to begin quilting with a knotted thread and when you want to hide the knot in the batting before taking any stitches. To make a foolproof knot, thread the needle with 18" to 24" of quilting thread. Draw the thread into a circle and hold with the eye of the needle between your right thumb and forefinger *(Diagram 30)*.

Wrap the thread around the needle two or three times with your left hand *(Diagram 31)*. Slide this coil of thread along the needle toward the eye until you can hold it, along with the eye and the thread end, in your right hand. Holding the eye of the needle with your left hand, use your right thumb and forefinger to slide the coil down the thread until it tightens

(Diagram 32). Trim any tail off the end. After a little practice, you will have a perfect knot every time.

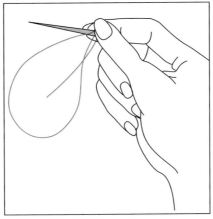

Diagram 30

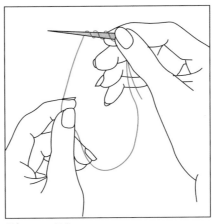

Diagram 31

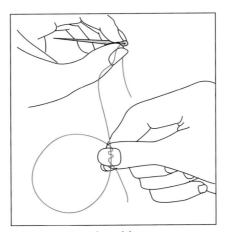

Diagram 32—Thread between thumb and forefinger

Quilting: Hand or Machine?

Quilting is the process of connecting the three layers with tiny running stitches. Many quilters find this stage the most rewarding and relaxing time spent with their project. The stitches add an all-important third dimension to your work by creating subtle shadows and nuances of depth that highlight the piecework. Two distinct forms of quilting, hand quilting and machine quilting, serve varying needs and accommodate a multitude of quilting requirements. For example, you might want to handquilt an heirloom quilt, but machine-quilt a crib quilt that may need to be washed often. Try both methods to discover the technique you like best.

Hand Quilting

Hand-quilted stitches should be evenly spaced, with the spaces between stitches about the same length as the stitches themselves. Although our goal is to have small, uniform stitches, the beauty of hand quilting is the human touch. Don't worry if you take only five or six stitches per inch; just be consistent throughout the quilt.

1. Start by placing your work in a frame or a hoop. Sit in a comfortable chair near a good light and have your thimble, scissors, thread, and quilting needles at hand. If you are right-handed, position yourself so that the line of quilting angles from upper right to lower left, so that you can quilt toward yourself. (Reverse these stitches if you are left-handed.)

2. To quilt, use a short needle called a "between". Betweens come in sizes 7 to 12, with 7 being the longest and 12 being the shortest. If you are a beginner, try a size 7 or 8. Because betweens are so much shorter than other sewing needles, they may feel awkward at first. (Also consider using a needle threader, even if you do not usually use one. The eye of a between is smaller than that of most needles and may be harder to thread.) As your skill increases, a smaller needle will help you make smaller stitches.

3. To keep your thread from snarling and knotting as you stitch, thread the needle before you cut the thread from the spool. Cut an 18"-24" length and make a small foolproof knot in the cut end (see page 29).

4. Insert the needle from the top of the quilt, about 1" from the beginning of the quilting line. Slide the needle through the batting, but do not pierce the backing. Bring the needle up at the beginning point and gently pull the thread; the knot will stop on the surface of the quilt. Tug the thread gently to pop the knot through the quilt top into the batting. If it does not slip through, use the point of the needle to gently separate the fabric threads and then tug again.

5. With your off hand under the quilt, insert the needle with the point straight down as shown in *Photo 1,* about ¹⁄₁₆" from the start. With your underneath finger, feel for the point as the needle comes through the backing. With a little practice, you will be able to find the point without pricking your finger.

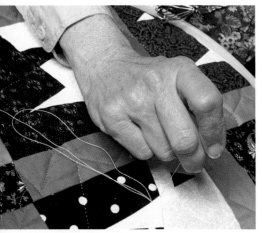

Photo 1

6. Push the fabric up from below as you rock the needle to a nearly horizontal position. Using the thumb of your sewing hand in conjunction with the off (underneath) hand, pinch a little hill in the fabric and push the tip of the needle back through the quilt top (see *Photo 2*).

Photo 2

7. You can push the needle all the way through to complete one stitch or rock the needle again to an upright position to take another stitch before pulling the needle through. At first, load only two or three stitches on the needle. As you gain experience, try more stitches at one time, but take no more than a quarter-needleful before pulling the needle through.

8. End the thread when you have 6" left. Tie a knot in the thread close to the quilt surface *(Diagram 33)*. Coming up with the needle about ½" from last stitch, pop the knot through the top *(Diagram 34)* and clip the tail. Rethread the needle and continue quilting. You should not be able to see where one thread ends and another begins, so no knots should be visible on the front or back.

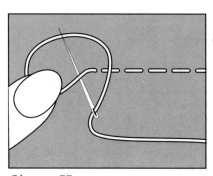

Diagram 33

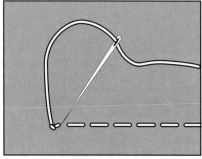

Diagram 34

Machine Quilting

For machine quilting, the backing and batting should be 3" larger all around than the quilt top, because the quilting process pushes the quilt top outward. After quilting, trim the backing and batting to the same size as the quilt top.

Thread your bobbin with good-quality sewing thread (not quilting thread) in a color to match the backing. Use a top thread color to match the quilt top or use invisible nylon thread.

An even-feed or walking foot will feed all the quilt's layers through the machine at the same speed. You can machine quilt without the walking foot by experimenting with tension adjustments and presser foot pressure. But, for a beginner, using the foot is much easier. If you do not have this foot, get one from your sewing machine dealer.

1. Roll both sides of the quilt toward the center. Leave a center section open, securing the rolled sides with quilt clips *(Diagram 35)*. These clips are sold in quilt shops and fabric stores.

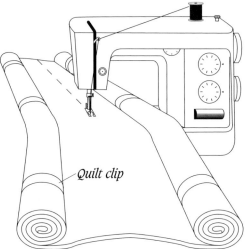

Quilt clip

Diagram 35

2. Start stitching at the center edge. Stitch in place several times to lock the stitches; or begin with a very short stitch and sew for about ½", gradually increasing the length to a setting of 12 stitches per inch.

3. Straight-line quilting is the easiest form of machine quilting. The seam lines for blocks and sashing should form a grid across the quilt. These are the longest lines of quilting, and they should be done first. Quilt down the center of the quilt, from one edge to the other.

4. Begin the next row at the bottom of the quilt. Alternating the directions of quilting lines will keep the layers from shifting. Continue quilting half of the quilt, unrolling it until you reach the edge.

5. Remove the quilt from the machine and reroll the completed side. Turn the quilt and work out from the center again to complete the quilting on the other side.

6. When you have completed the vertical quilting lines, reroll the quilt in the other direction to quilt the horizontal lines. Start in the center and proceed in the same manner.

7. Some quilts do not have vertical and horizontal quilting lines. Instead, the lines may be diagonal or follow the design of the patchwork. Always machine-quilt the longest lines first, starting at the center edge.

8. Use a darning foot for free-motion quilting to make curved lines or fancy designs. Drop the feed dogs so that you will be able to move the quilt freely without turning it. An embroidery or quilting hoop is useful to keep the fabric flat and to provide the right amount of tension while quilting. To move to a new unquilted area, drop the needle into the fabric, shift the hoop, and continue quilting. I find machine quilting in smaller areas, as in *Fan Flowers* (page 80), very satisfying because I don't have to contend with all the bulk.

Binding the Quilt

You have taken that last loving quilting stitch. Now you are ready to bind the quilt. I prefer a double-fold bias binding, made by sewing a bias tube and cutting continuous bias binding. In some instances,

I use straight-of-the-grain binding, connecting the strips with a 45° diagonal seam. A standard width to cut is 2½", which you then press in half lengthwise.

Continuous Bias Binding Formula

To determine the amount of fabric you need to make continuous bias binding, first find the perimeter of the quilt by adding the lengths of all four sides. Multiply the perimeter by the desired width of the binding. Using a calculator, find the square root ($\sqrt{\ }$) of that figure. The result is the size of the square of fabric required to make enough binding for your quilt. I sometimes add an extra 2" to ensure that I have enough. (If you prefer to use purchased binding, simply divide the perimeter by 36" for the number of yards of binding to buy.)

Making Continuous Bias Binding

To make continuous bias binding, cut the square in half diagonally to make two triangles. With right sides facing and raw edges aligned, place the two triangles together and stitch (indicated as Seam 1, *Diagram 36*). Press the seam allowance open.

Mark the unit with parallel lines the desired width of the binding *(Diagram 37)*, taking care not to stretch the bias edges. With right sides facing, align the short raw edges (indicated as Seam 2 in *Diagram 38*). As you align the edges, offset one Seam 2 point past its natural matching point by one line. Stitch the seam; then press the seam allowance open.

Cut the binding in a continuous strip, starting with the protruding point and following the marked lines around the tube *(Diagram 38)*. Press the strip in half lengthwise with wrong sides facing.

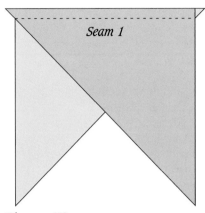

Diagram 36

Diagram 37

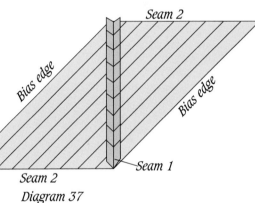

Diagram 38

Applying Binding

To apply the binding, begin anywhere on the edge of the quilt, except at the corner. Make a diagonal cut at one end of the binding. Matching raw edges, pin the binding on the quilt top. Start stitching 2" from the diagonal cut *(Diagram 39)*. Machine-stitch the binding to the quilt, using a ¼" seam. Stop stitching ¼" from the corner, backstitch, and break off thread. Fold the binding strip diagonally away from the quilt, making a 45° angle *(Diagram 40)*.

Fold the binding strip straight down along the next side to be stitched, creating a pleat in the corner.

Position the needle at the ¼" seam line of the new side *(Diagram 41)*. Make a few stitches, backstitch, and then stitch the seam. Continue until all corners and sides are done. When you reach the starting point, trim the excess binding at a 45° angle, opened flat to coincide with the initial cut plus ½". Sew this diagonal seam, refold, and finish binding.

Turn the binding over the raw edge of the quilt. Slipstitch it in place on the back, using thread that matches the binding.

At each corner, fold the binding to form a miter *(Diagram 42)*. Hand-stitch the miters closed if desired.

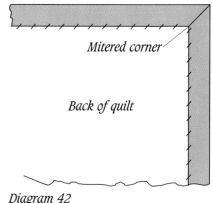

Mitered corner

Back of quilt

Diagram 42

Making a Hanging Sleeve

Quilts that are hung for wall display should have a sleeve attached to the back. A dowel, curtain rod, or lattice board, slipped through the sleeve, can hang from brackets on the wall.

1. Cut a 6"-wide fabric piece that measures the width of the quilt plus 2". Turn under a ¼" hem on each end and press; then turn under 1" more. Press and topstitch.

2. With wrong sides facing, join long edges. Press the seam allowances open, centering the seam on one side of the tube. With the seam facing the quilt backing, place the sleeve just below the binding at the top of the quilt, centering it between the quilt sides *(Diagram 43)*.

3. Slipstitch the top and bottom edges of the sleeve to the quilt backing only, making sure no stitches go through the quilt top.

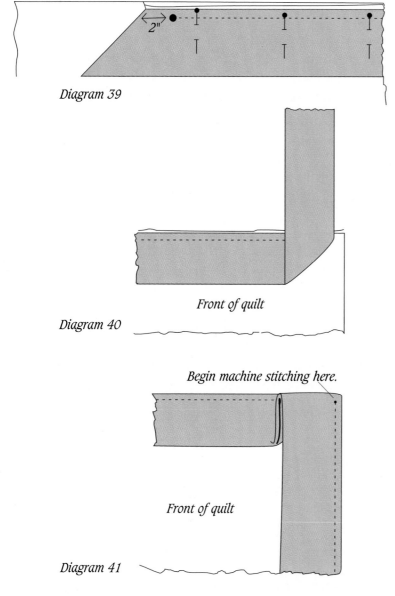

Diagram 39

Diagram 40

Front of quilt

Begin machine stitching here.

Front of quilt

Diagram 41

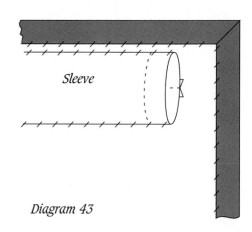

Sleeve

Diagram 43

My son, Paul, has captured the essence of quilt-making in the words from this song, "Quilts." In it, he tells how quilts bring people together and how meaningful our cloth interaction has become. It is now the theme song for my Lap Quilting television series. How better to convey the true meaning of quilting than with verse and song!

Quilts

Could you imagine a more clever object?
Warms the body, ignites the mind.
Brings two people together for
The essentials of nature,
Puts them to bed one day at a time.
The art of the heart and design of the mind.
Given as gifts since the animal hide,
Warms the body, ignites the mind.
A child sleeps under a mother's creation.
Together forever, past and present sewn
      in a relation.
The art of the heart and design of the mind.
Softer and drier than a baby's bottom,
Put together with your hands of time.
Could you imagine a more clever object?
The art of the heart and design of the mind.
Reach deep down as far as you can find,
To pull some magic out for your next design.
Just when you think that it's hopeless once again,
Your vision comes and it's dancing with the wind.
The art of the heart and design of the mind.

Paul Bonesteel, 1994

on the cutting edge

Rodeo Roundup

Baby Cowpoke

King-sized Cowpoke

Calico Crossover

Log Cabin Spin Wall Hanging

Quilt of Many Friends

Pillow Collection

Equilateral Love

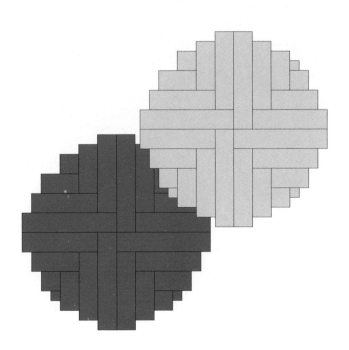

Rodeo Roundup

Rodeo Roundup

Novelty fabrics are great! Wonderful prints in today's shops offer many themes from which to choose. I had fun working with Western motifs—horses, cowboys, coyotes, and more.

Finished Size
Blocks: 112 (5⅝") blocks
Quilt: 80" x 80"

Easy-Does-It Feature: Quick-pieced half-square triangles

Materials
2⅜ yards lightweight dark blue denim for outer border and binding
1 yard striped fabric for inner border
⅝ yard *each* of 4 shades lightweight denim
9¼" squares 28 assorted print fabrics
4¾ yards fabric for backing or 2½ yards 90"-wide fabric

Cutting
Cut all strips cross-grain except borders as noted.
From **dark blue denim**, cut:
4 (5½" x 80½") lengthwise strips for outer border.
8 (9¼") squares.
   Cut each square in quarters diagonally to get 4 triangles from each square, for a total of 32 triangles.
From **striped fabric**, cut:
9 yards 3½"-wide bias.
   See page 31 for instructions on cutting continuous bias. From continuous bias, cut 4 (71"-long) strips for inner border.
From **4 shades of denim**, cut:
28 (9¼") squares total.

Quick Piecing Triangle-Squares
1. With right sides facing, match each 9¼" print square with a denim square. Stitch around all sides of each pair, ¼" from edge *(Diagram 1)*.

2. Cut each square in quarters diagonally as shown to get 4 triangle-squares from each pair.

3. Press all seams toward print fabrics. (*Note:* Handle blocks carefully as outer edges are bias and will stretch.) Trim dog-ears.

Quilt Top Assembly
1. Referring to *Diagram 2,* arrange 28 blocks in 7 horizontal rows to make a quarter-section. (Medium blue triangles indicate denim fabrics.) Add a dark blue triangle to end of each row. Join rows, adding 1 dark blue triangle at bottom to complete triangular quarter-section. Make 4 sections.

2. Referring to *Quilt Top Assembly Diagram,* arrange quarter-sections with dark blue triangles on outer edge. Join 2 pairs of adjacent sections; then join halves.

3. Matching centers of borders and quilt sides, sew bias-cut striped borders to each side of quilt top. Stitch with bias strips against feed dogs. Miter border corners.

4. Add dark blue borders to quilt top in same manner.

Quilting and Finishing
1. Layer backing, batting, and quilt top. Quilt as desired. Quilt shown is machine-quilted in an all-over pattern.

2. From remaining dark blue denim, make 330" of bias or straight-grain binding. See page 31 for directions on binding.

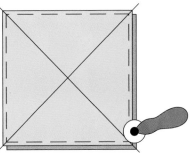

Diagram 1

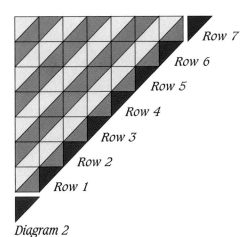

Row 7
Row 6
Row 5
Row 4
Row 3
Row 2
Row 1

Diagram 2

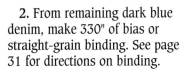

Quilt Top Assembly Diagram

Baby Cowpoke

Baby Cowpoke

Scraps are fun, but I like a structured look, too. So I adapted the basic idea of *Rodeo Roundup* (page 37) to make a crib quilt with just two fabrics. Sticking to my Western theme, I combined a cowboy toile with dark blue denim. I started with smaller squares than for the full-size quilt, so the same procedure results in a smaller quilt that is made rectangular with extra rows at the top and bottom.

Finished Size
Blocks: 142 ($2\frac{7}{8}$") blocks
Quilt: 45" x 53"

Easy-Does-It Feature: Quick-pieced half-square triangles

Materials
$1\frac{3}{4}$ yards print fabric
$1\frac{1}{2}$ yards lightweight dark blue denim
$\frac{7}{8}$ yard red print fabric for inner border and binding
$1\frac{1}{2}$ yards fabric for backing or $1\frac{3}{8}$ yards 54"-wide fabric
Red embroidery floss or pearl cotton

Cutting
Cut all strips cross-grain except middle and outer borders as noted.
From **print fabric,** cut:
   2 (3" x $53\frac{1}{2}$") lengthwise strips and 2 (3" x $45\frac{1}{2}$") lengthwise strips for outer border.
   45 ($5\frac{1}{4}$") squares.
      Cut 8 of these squares in quarters diagonally to get 4 triangles from each square, for a total of 32 triangles.
From **dark blue denim,** cut:
   2 ($1\frac{1}{2}$" x $48\frac{1}{2}$") lengthwise strips and 2 ($1\frac{1}{2}$" x $40\frac{1}{2}$") strips for middle border.
   37 ($5\frac{1}{4}$") squares.
From **red fabric,** cut:
   2 ($3\frac{1}{2}$" x $38\frac{1}{2}$") strips and 4 ($3\frac{1}{2}$" x 24") strips for inner border.

Quilt Top Assembly
   1. See *Rodeo Roundup* instructions, page 37, to make 146 triangle-square blocks.
   2. Referring to *Diagram 1,* arrange 28 blocks in 7 horizontal rows to make a quarter-section. (Dark blue triangles indicate denim.) Add 1 print triangle to end of each row as shown. Join rows, adding 1 print triangle at bottom as shown to complete quarter-section. Make 2 of these sections.
   3. In a similar manner, arrange 45 blocks in 9 horizontal rows as shown in *Diagram 2.* At ends of rows 1 and 9, trim corner triangle-squares as shown. (Be sure to leave $\frac{1}{4}$" seam allowance.) Make 2 of these sections.

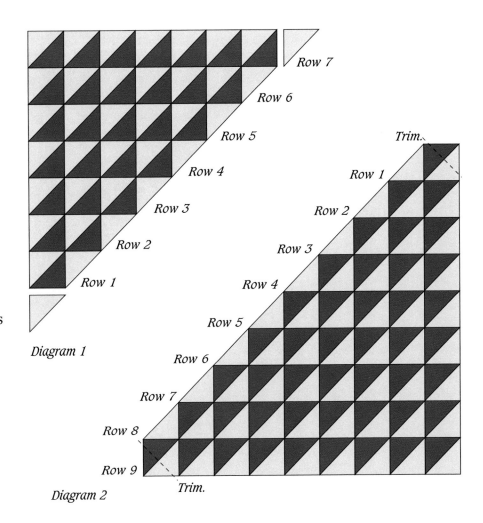

Row 7
Row 6
Row 5
Row 4
Row 3
Row 2
Row 1

Diagram 1

Trim.
Row 1
Row 2
Row 3
Row 4
Row 5
Row 6
Row 7
Row 8
Row 9
Trim.

Diagram 2

4. Arrange quarter-sections as shown in *Quilt Top Assembly Diagram.* Join each pair of adjacent sections; then join halves.

5. Join 24"-long strips of red fabric to make 2 side borders 46½" long. Matching centers of borders and quilt sides, sew red borders to edges of quilt. Miter border corners.

6. Add dark blue borders, mitering corners. Then add print borders in same manner.

Quilting and Finishing

1. Layer backing, batting, and quilt top. Quilt as desired. Quilt shown is tied with red floss at center of each block, with additional machine quilting in outer border.

2. From remaining red fabric, make 200" of bias or straight-grain binding. See page 31 for directions on making and applying binding.

Quilt Top Assembly Diagram

gem from georgia

Because they stretch, bias edges on the perimeter of a quilt invite disaster. To avoid stretching the quilt out of shape, be sure to cut pieces so outside edges are on the straight of the grain.

King-sized Cowpoke

To get maximum impact from my novelty prints, I cut even larger squares to start off this Texas-size version of *Rodeo Roundup*, page 37. This quilt shows another effect you can achieve by varying placement of light and dark fabrics. Have fun! Experiment with block size, fabrics, and colors until your quilt is just the way you want it!

Finished Size
Blocks: 128 (8½") blocks
Quilt: 96" x 108"

Materials
1⅛ yards *each* of 4 shades light-weight denim
13¼" squares 36 assorted print fabrics
1 yard red fabric for binding
9 yards fabric for backing or 3¼ yards 108"-wide fabric

Quilt Top Assembly
Following instructions for *Rodeo Roundup* on page 37, cut 37 (13¼") squares of denim. Use 32 squares each of denim and print fabrics to make 128 triangle-squares. Cut each remaining square into 4 triangles. Referring to photo below, follow *Rodeo Roundup* instructions to assemble quilt, adding an extra row to top and bottom quarter-sections (as in *Baby Cowpoke,* page 39).

King-sized Cowpoke

Calico Crossover

42

Calico Crossover

I began with the idea of specific placement for each of the 24 scrap fabrics in this quilt, but found I liked it better when everything got all mixed up. So I let serendipity arrange the red, pink, and purple fabrics. By turning blocks to align light and dark, the fabrics create an illusion of interlocked squares. Making this quilt can be even faster using just two alternating fabrics against a solid background.

Finished Size
Blocks: 12 (20") blocks
Quilt: 80" x 100"

Easy-Does-It Feature: Strip piecing

Materials
11" x 14" *each* of 12 light and 12
    dark scrap fabrics*
2¾ yards muslin
2¾ yards striped fabric for border
⅜ yard contrasting solid fabric for
    border
1 yard fabric for binding
6 yards fabric for backing or 3 yards
    90"-wide fabric
*If using just 2 fabrics, buy 1⅜ yards
    of each.

Cutting
Cut all strips cross-grain except as noted.
From *each* **scrap fabric,** cut:
    1 (8½" x 10") strip.
    2 (2½" x 10") strips.
From **muslin,** cut:
    21 (2½" x 42") strips.
        From these, cut 84 (2½" x 10") strips.
    6 (6½" x 42") strips.
        From these, cut 24 (6½" x 10") strips.
From **striped fabric,** cut:
    2 (2" x 60½") lengthwise strips
        and 2 (2" x 80½") lengthwise
        strips for inner border.
    4 (8" x 42") strips and 6 (8" x 36")
        strips for outer border.
From **solid border fabric,** cut:
    8 (1½"-wide) strips for middle border.

Piecing Blocks
1. Group the 3 strips of 1 light scrap with the 3 strips of a compatible dark scrap to make 1 light/dark combination. Repeat to make 12 light/dark fabric combinations.
2. Referring to *strip set diagrams,* join strips of 1 combination with muslin strips to make 1 each of strip sets 1, 2, 3, 4, and 5.
3. On Strip Set 3, press seam allowances toward print fabrics. On other strip sets, press seam allowances toward muslin.
4. From *each* strip set, cut 4 (2½"-wide) segments.
5. Referring to *Quarter Block Assembly Diagram,* join 1 segment from each strip set (in numerical order) to make 1 quarter block. Press seam allowances toward strips 2 and 4. Repeat with remaining strip-set segments to make 3 more quarter blocks.
6. Repeat steps 2–5 with each light/dark combination until you have 48 quarter blocks (4 of each fabric combination).
7. Lay out quarter blocks in groups of 4, arranging them as shown in *Block Assembly Diagram.* Experiment with different groupings to maximize effects of light and dark fabric combinations. For each block, join quarter blocks in pairs as shown. Join pairs to complete 1 block, twirling center seams (see page 23). Press block.
8. Repeat to make 11 more blocks.

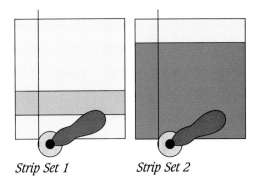

Strip Set 1   *Strip Set 2*

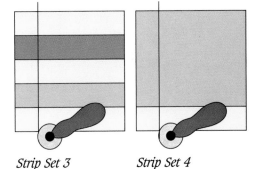

Strip Set 3   *Strip Set 4*

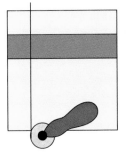

Strip Set 5

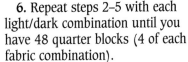

1   2   3   4   5
Quarter Block Assembly Diagram

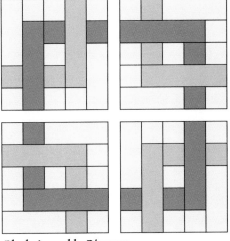

Block Assembly Diagram

43

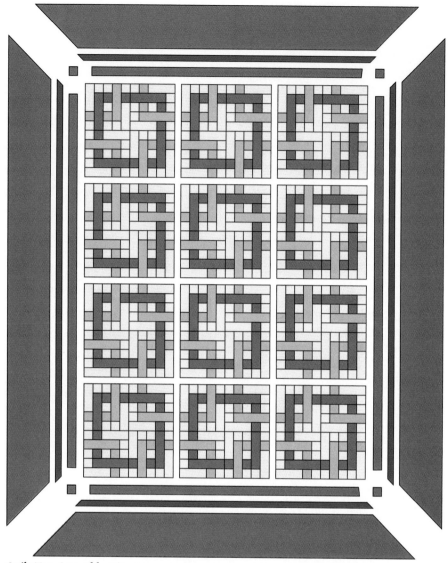

Quilt Top Assembly Diagram

Quilt Top Assembly

1. Referring to *Quilt Top Assembly Diagram,* join blocks in 4 horizontal rows of 3 blocks each. Join rows.

2. For inner borders, join 2" x 60½" strips of striped fabric to top and bottom edges. Press seam allowances toward borders.

3. From remaining dark scraps, cut 4 (2") squares. Join a square to both ends of each 80½"-long inner border. Join these borders to quilt sides.

4. For middle borders, join 1½"-wide strips of solid fabric to make 2 (1½" x 65½") borders for top and bottom edges. Make 2 (1½" x 85½") borders for sides. Join borders to quilt; then miter corners.

5. For outer borders, join 8" x 42" strips of striped fabric to make 2 (8" x 80½") borders for top and bottom edges. Join 8" x 36" strips to make 2 (8" x 100½") borders for sides. Join borders to quilt; then miter corners.

Quilting and Finishing

1. Make a stencil for heart quilting design. Mark design on each quarter block, overlapping hearts as shown in *Quilting Diagram.* Mark quilting designs on borders as desired.

2. Layer backing, batting, and quilt top. Quilt as desired.

3. Make 370" of bias or straight-grain binding. See page 31 for directions on making and applying binding.

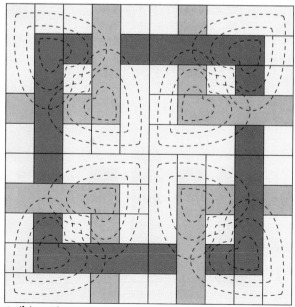

Quilting Diagram

Place on fold.

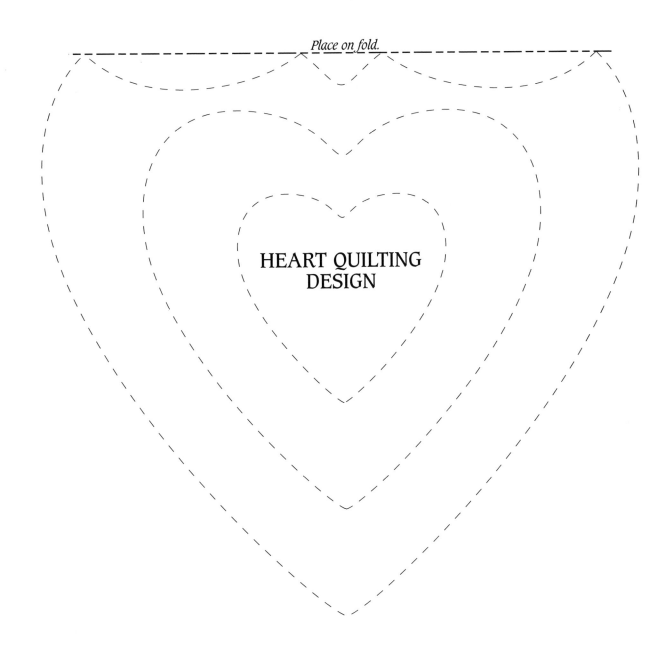

HEART QUILTING
DESIGN

Log Cabin Spin Wall Hanging

gem from georgia

It's fun to create a design in which blocks appear to overlap, like these Log Cabin circles. Changing the length and width of the strips used to make the traditional block will form circles when you join the blocks.

Log Cabin Spin Wall Hanging

The classic Log Cabin block is updated! Using different strip widths makes an asymmetrical block, although the block is sewn like any Log Cabin. When four asymmetrical blocks come together, they create the illusion of a circle. For this wall hanging, Barbara Swinea chose batik-like fabrics for the circles, which float across a field of muted Log Cabin blocks. Barbara patterned her quilt after one designed by Jodie Stutchbury and made by the Five Directions group for the governor's western residence in Asheville, North Carolina.

Finished Size
Blocks: 117 (5") blocks
Wall Hanging: 45" x 65"
Note: To make a twin-sized quilt, see tip on page 49.

Easy-Does-It Feature: Chain piecing

Materials
2 yards solid navy fabric
1¼ yards solid light gray fabric
1 yard solid dark gray fabric
¼ yard *each* of 14 prints for circles
¾ yard fabric for binding
3 yards fabric for backing or 1 yard
     108"-wide fabric

Cutting
   Cut all strips cross-grain.
From **navy fabric,** cut:
   70 (1"-wide) strips.
From **light gray fabric,** cut:
   36 (1"-wide) strips.
From **dark gray fabric,** cut:
   30 (1"-wide) strips.
From *each* **print fabric,** cut:
   1 (1"-wide) strip.
   2 (1½"-wide) strips.

Piecing Basic Log Cabin Blocks
   Block A is a basic Log Cabin block, made with strips of the same width.

   1. Referring to *Diagram 1,* join a strip of light gray fabric to a navy strip. Press seam allowances toward navy fabric. From this strip set, cut 36 (1"-wide) units as shown for block centers.

   2. Positioning gray and navy fabrics as shown, chain-piece segments to navy strips as shown in *Diagram 2.* Press seam allowances toward navy strip; then cut segments apart.

   3. Following *Block A1 diagram,* continue to chain-piece logs, increasing the block size as logs are added to each side. Always press seam allowance toward newest log. Complete 36 blocks.

   4. Repeating steps 1–3, make 32 blocks with navy and dark gray fabrics *(Block A2 diagram).*

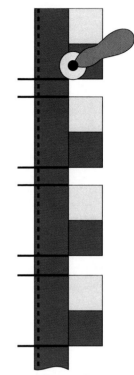

Diagram 2

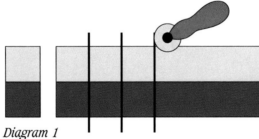

Diagram 1

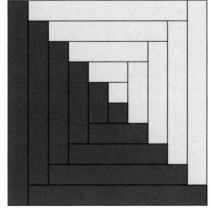

Block A1

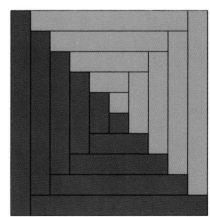

Block A2

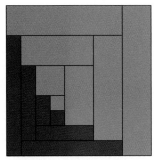

Block B

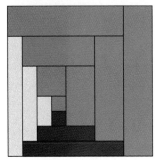

Block C

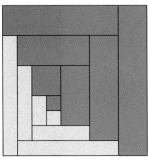

Block D

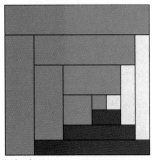

Block E

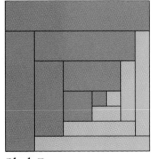

Block F

Piecing Blocks for Circles

Blocks for circles are made in the same manner as basic Log Cabin blocks. Because there are at most 4 blocks made the same way, strip piecing and chain piecing are not efficient here. Each block starts with a 1"-wide square of print fabric; then 1½"-wide print strips are used alternately with the solid strips. This gives you finished logs ½" and 1" wide. Refer to diagrams for blocks B, C, D, E, and F to make blocks.

Assign 1 print fabric to each circle. For placement and relationships of adjacent circles, refer to *Quilt Top Assembly Diagram.*

1. For Circle 1, make 4 of Block B.

2. For Circle 2, make 2 of Block B and 1 of Block C. For fourth block, make 1 of Block D, substituting dark gray fabric for light gray shown in block diagram.

3. For Circle 3, make 1 of Block C and 1 of Block E. Remaining 2 blocks are shared with circles 4 and 5.

4. For Circle 4, make 1 each of blocks B, D, and E. For fourth block, make 1 Block F, using Circle 3 fabric for narrow strips.

5. For Circle 5, make 1 each of blocks C and D and 2 of Block F, using print fabrics from circles 3 and 6 for narrow strips.

6. For Circle 6, make 3 of Block E, substituting dark gray fabric for light gray shown. Fourth block is shared with Circle 5.

7. For Circle 7, make 1 each of blocks B, C, D, and E.

8. For Circle 8, make 2 of Block B and 1 of Block C. For fourth block, make 1 Block F, using Circle 9 fabric for narrow strips.

9. For Circle 9, make 1 each of blocks B and D. Two remaining blocks are shared with circles 8 and 10.

10. For Circle 10, make 1 each of blocks B, C, and D. For fourth block, make 1 Block F, using Circle 9 fabric for narrow strips.

11. For Circle 11, make 1 each of blocks C, D, and E. Fourth block is shared with Circle 12.

12. For Circle 12, make 1 each of blocks C, D, and E. For fourth block, make 1 Block F, using Circle 11 fabric for narrow strips.

13. For Circle 13, make 1 each of blocks C, D, and E. Fourth block is shared with Circle 14.

14. For Circle 14, make 1 each of blocks C, D, and E. For fourth block, make 1 Block F, using Circle 13 fabric for narrow strips.

Quilt Top Assembly

The essential ingredient in putting blocks together correctly is space to lay out all 117 blocks. If you have a felt-covered wall or large board, stick the blocks up in place. For most people, the floor is the best area. Follow *Quilt Top Assembly Diagram* closely throughout.

1. Referring to diagram, lay out blocks in 9 horizontal rows of 13 blocks each. Note that blocks with dark gray fabric are all on outer edge. Turn blocks so fabrics are positioned correctly. In most cases, you are matching the same fabrics in adjacent blocks. When satisfied with layout, it is a good idea to mark the top of each block with a pin to avoid confusion when carrying block pairs to the sewing machine.

2. Join blocks in horizontal rows as shown. Return rows to layout as you complete them and recheck block position before you proceed.

3. Join rows to complete quilt top.

Quilting and Finishing

1. Layer backing, batting, and quilt top. Quilt as desired. Quilt shown is hand-quilted through middle of each print log. The remainder of wall hanging is quilted in a pattern of concentric circles and semi-circles.

2. Make 225" of bias or straight-grain binding. See page 31 for directions on making and applying binding.

3. See page 32 for tips on making a hanging sleeve.

Quilt Top Assembly Diagram
(Letters indicate blocks. Numbers indicate circles.)

Cut wider strips to make a twin-size quilt with a finished size of 67½" x 97½". Instead of the strip widths listed, cut all navy and gray strips 1¼" wide. Cut print strips 1¼" wide and 2" wide. The finished size of the block will be 7½" square.

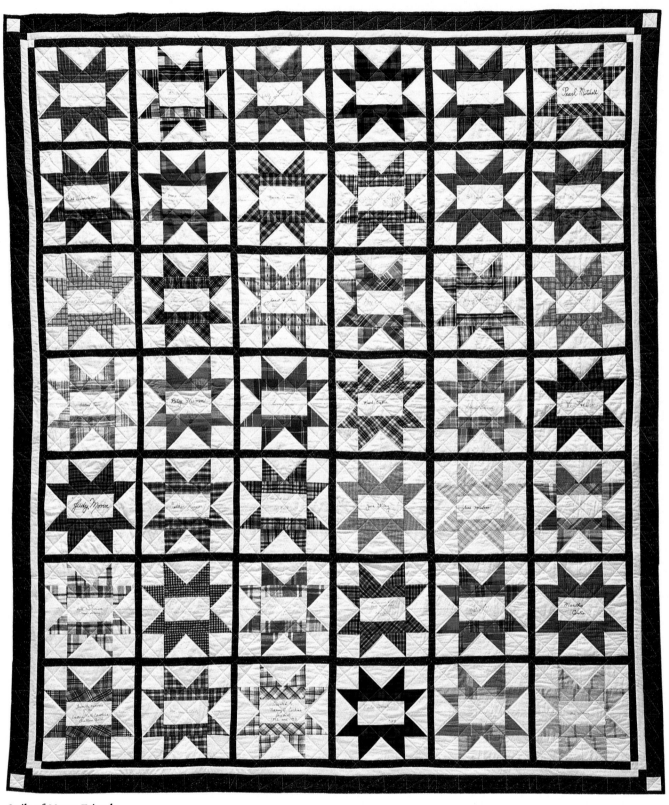

Quilt of Many Friends

50

Quilt of Many Friends

A guild president who holds office for two consecutive terms deserves a *Quilt of Many Friends*. Members of the Western North Carolina Quilters Guild made this plaid tribute for their president, Nancy Cochran. From the time the newsletter carried the autograph star pattern to all but Nancy, the project was hush-hush until the meeting when the results were unfurled.

Finished Size
Blocks: 42 (12") blocks
Quilt: 85" x 98"

Easy-Does-It Feature: Quick-pieced half-square triangle squares

Materials
4⅔ yards muslin for stars and middle border
3¼ yards dark fabric for borders, sashing, and binding
9" x 12" scrap plaid fabric for *each* star
6 yards fabric for backing or 3 yards 90"-wide fabric
Freezer paper
Permanent fabric marker

Cutting
Cut all strips cross-grain.
From **muslin,** cut:
9 (1½"-wide) strips.
From each of 4 of these, cut 1 (1½") square for inner border corners. Set aside remaining strips for middle border.

21 (3½"-wide) strips.
From these, cut 168 (3½") squares for block corners and 42 (3½" x 6½") rectangles for block centers.
9 (7¾"-wide) strips.
From these, cut 42 (7¾") squares for half-square triangles.
4 (2½") squares for outer border corners.
From **dark fabric,** cut:
33 (1½"-wide) strips.
Set aside 21 strips for horizontal sashing and inner border.
From remaining strips, cut 35 (1½" x 12½") vertical sashing strips and 4 (1½") squares for middle border corners.
9 (2½"-wide) strips for outer borders.
From *each* **plaid fabric,** cut:
1 (7¾") square.
2 (2" x 6½") rectangles.

Quick Piecing Triangle-Squares
1. Referring to *Diagram 1*, draw 2 diagonal lines from corner to corner on wrong side of 1 (7¾") muslin square. Draw vertical and horizontal lines through center of square as shown.
2. With right sides facing, align muslin square atop 1 plaid square.
3. Stitch ¼" seam on *both* sides of each diagonal line as shown.
4. Cut on all drawn lines to get 8 triangle-squares.
5. On 4 triangle-squares, press seam allowances toward muslin. Press toward plaid on remaining 4 squares. Trim dog-ears.

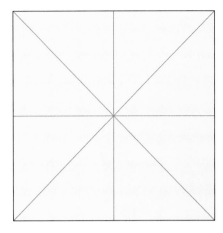

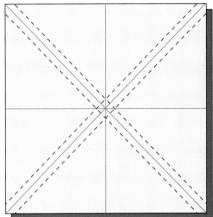

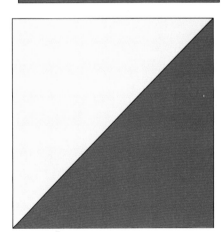

Diagram 1

gem from georgia

I recommend a product called Pro Retayne as a fixative for print fabric that continues to fade. Colors are permanently set once the fabric is washed in this solution. Look for this product in quilt shops and fabric stores.

Piecing Blocks

1. It is best to sign center rectangles before sewing. Backing pieces with freezer paper stabilizes them for writing and keeps signatures from going into seam allowances. Cut a 3" x 6" rectangle of freezer paper for each muslin rectangle. Center freezer paper, coated side down, on back of fabric and press with warm iron. Remove freezer paper when writing is complete.

2. Referring to *Diagram 2,* join 2 triangle-squares on muslin sides, combining squares whose seams are pressed in opposite directions. Repeat with remaining triangle-squares to make 3 more rectangles.

3. To make top and bottom rows of block, sew a 3½" muslin square to sides of pieced triangles as shown in *Block Assembly Diagram.*

4. Referring to *Block Assembly Diagram,* sew 2 rectangles of same plaid to sides of muslin center rectangle. Join pieced rectangles to sides of center square as shown to complete middle row.

5. Join rows to complete star block.

6. Repeating quick piecing with each square of plaid fabric, make 42 star blocks.

Quilt Top Assembly

Refer to *Quilt Top Assembly Diagram* throughout assembly.

1. Arrange blocks in 7 horizontal rows of 6 blocks each.

2. Join blocks in each row, sewing a sashing strip between blocks as shown in *Row Assembly Diagram.*

3. For horizontal sashing, join 2 (1½"-wide) strips of dark fabric. Trim strip ends until sashing matches length of your block row (approximately 77½"). Make 8 strips of horizontal sashing.

4. Join rows, sewing horizontal sashing between rows. Add 2 remaining sashing rows to top and bottom of quilt for inner border.

5. From remaining 1½"-wide dark strips, piece 2 (90½"-long) side borders. Join a muslin square to both ends of each border; then join borders to quilt sides.

6. From 1½"-wide muslin strips, piece 2 (79½"-long) borders and 2 (92½"-long) borders. Trim borders to fit quilt top. Join shorter borders to top and bottom of quilt. Sew 1½" dark squares to ends of long borders; then sew these borders to quilt sides.

7. From 2½"-wide dark strips, piece 2 (81½"-long) borders and 2 (94½"-long) borders. Trim and join these to quilt in same manner, adding 2½" muslin squares to ends of long border strips.

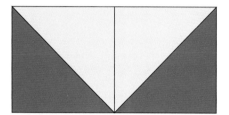

Diagram 2

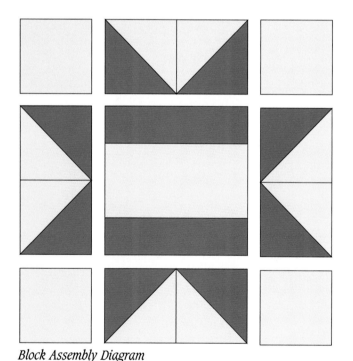

Block Assembly Diagram

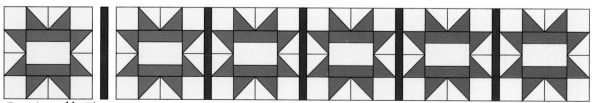

Row Assembly Diagram

Quilting and Finishing

1. Layer backing, batting, and quilt top. Quilt as desired. Quilt shown is machine-quilted following diagonal lines of stars.

2. From remaining dark fabric, make 372" of bias or straight-grain binding. See page 31 for directions on making and applying binding.

Quilt Top Assembly Diagram

Twirl

Spin-Off

54

Pillow Collection

Make a color splash to brighten any room with patchwork pillows. Bold black and sunny yellow frame each member of this trio of quick cut-and-stitch designs. Each pillow is finished with a lapped back.

Finished Size
Blocks: 12" square
Pillows: 18" square

Easy-Does-It Feature: Partial seams

Materials for *each* pillow
⅝ yard solid yellow fabric for outer border and back
⅛ yard black checked or striped fabric for inner border*
Assorted bright-colored scraps (see instructions for colors)
18½" square muslin for quilting
18½" square batting
18"-square pillow form
*Additional fabric will be needed if you choose to cut bias strips.

Cutting (for *each* pillow)
Cut scraps as listed for each block.
From **yellow fabric**, cut:
2 (13½" x 18½") pieces for pillow back.
4 (2½" x 18½") strips for outer border.
From **black checked or striped fabric,** cut:
4 (1½" x 14½") strips for inner border.

Piecing Indian Trail Block
Refer to *Indian Trail Block Assembly Diagram* throughout.

1. From 16 assorted fabric scraps, cut 4 (2½") squares for center block, 8 (2½" x 4½") rectangles for sides, and 4 (4½") squares for corners.

2. Join small squares to make a four-patch for center block.

3. Join rectangles in pairs as shown.

4. Join units in horizontal rows as shown.

5. Join 3 rows to complete block.

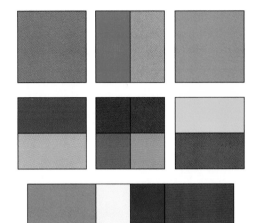

Indian Trail Block Assembly Diagram

Indian Trail

gem
from
georgia

Does your presser foot measure a precise ¼" seam allowance? Use graph paper with a ¼" grid to find out. Place paper under the presser foot and drop the needle down through a line on the paper. Look where the next line is in relationship to the right side of the foot. If it's not precisely aligned, mark the ¼" line on your throatplate.

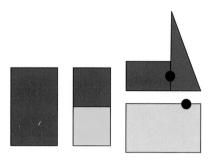

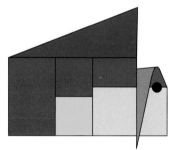

Diagram 1

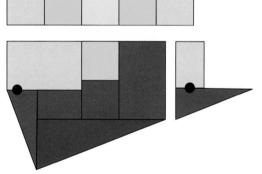

Diagram 2

Diagram 3

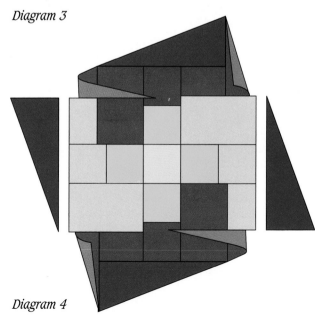

Diagram 4

Piecing Twirl Block

1. From pink fabric, cut 2 (3" x 4½") rectangles, 2 (2" x 2⅞") rectangles, and 2 (2½") squares. Cut same pieces from red fabric. Cut 4 (2½") squares of gold fabric and 1 (2½") square of yellow fabric.

2. From purple fabric, cut 2 (2⅜" x 5⅞") rectangles. From blue fabric, cut 2 (3⅜" x 8⅝") rectangles. Cut each rectangle in half diagonally to get 4 triangles of each color. Trim 1" from tip of all 8 triangles.

3. Join red squares to gold squares. Referring to *Diagram 1,* join a large red rectangle to 1 side of each 2-square unit.

4. Join purple triangle to 1 end of small red rectangle with a partial seam, leaving ¼" unsewn at top of joining seam. Backstitch. (*Note:* Dots on diagrams denote partial seams.) Sew this unit to 1 side of large pink rectangle with partial seam in same manner as shown. Backstitch.

5. Folding purple triangle out of the way, join large blue triangle to top of unit as shown in *Diagram 2.* Matching right sides with end of blue triangle, turn purple triangle down and complete partial seam. Make 2 units as shown in *Diagram 2.*

6. Join remaining purple triangles to small pink rectangles with partial seam as shown in *Diagram 3.* Join these to sides of each unit as shown.

7. Join remaining squares in a row as shown in *Diagram 3.*

8. Referring to *Diagram 4,* join units with 5-square row in center.

9. Folding partial-seamed purple triangles out of the way, join blue triangles to sides as shown in *Diagram 4.* Then finish seams of purple triangles.

Piecing Spin-Off Block

Refer to *Spin-Off Block Assembly Diagram* throughout.

1. From scraps of at least 9 assorted fabrics, cut 13 (2⅝") squares (A) and 4 (2⅝" x 6⅞") rectangles (B). Cut 3 (4¼") squares. Cut these into quarters diagonally to form 12 triangles (C). Cut 2 (2⅜") squares. Cut these in half diagonally to form 4 triangles (D).

2. Follow *Spin-Off Block Assembly Diagram* to join pieces A–D to form pillow block.

Adding Borders

Referring to *Border Assembly Diagram,* sew a strip of checked or striped fabric to each side of block, making square or mitered corners as desired. Sew yellow border strips to block sides in same manner.

Quilting and Finishing

1. Layer pillow top over batting and muslin. Baste.

2. Quilt pillow as desired.

3. To make lapped back, turn under a ¼" hem on 1 long edge of *each* 13½" x 18½" yellow rectangle and press. Turn under another ¼" and topstitch.

4. With right sides facing and matching raw edges on 3 sides, lay 1 rectangle over 1 end of quilted pillow top. Lay second rectangle over opposite end of pillow in same manner, overlapping hemmed edges at center. Stitch around all 4 sides.

5. Clip seam allowances at corners. Turn pillow top right side out and insert pillow form.

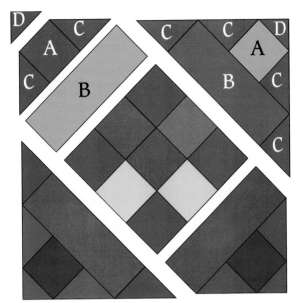

Spin-Off Block Assembly Diagram

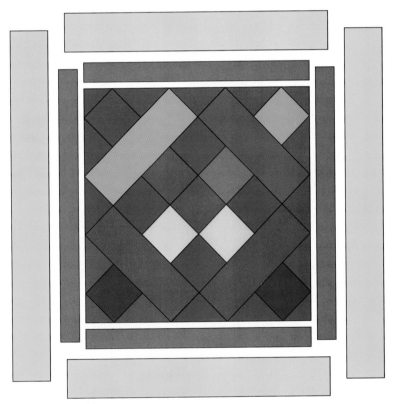

Border Assembly Diagram

Equilateral Love

58

Equilateral Love

I just *love* plaids, so I knew they'd make a handsome homespun quilt. Variety gives the quilt a scrappy look, but the fabric placement is not as random as it may seem. Concentric rings of red, green, and blue radiate outward from a center star. For the version shown in the photograph, I chose to sprinkle bits of yellow, white, black, and brown here and there for accent.

Finished Size
Quilt: 81" x 102"

Easy-Does-It Feature: Rotary cutting 60° angles

Materials
- 11 (¼-yard) pieces assorted red plaids
- 13 (¼-yard) pieces assorted green plaids
- 12 (¼-yard) pieces assorted blue plaids
- 1½ yards dark red print fabric for outer border
- ⅝ yard white print fabric for inner border
- ⅞ yard fabric for binding
- 6 yards fabric for backing or 3 yards 90"-wide fabric

Cutting
Cut all strips cross-grain. Refer to *Cutting Diagram* on page 60 to cut equilateral triangles and half-triangles from strips, using ruler as described on page 24 or using templates made from patterns on page 61. You should be able to cut 12 triangles and 2 half-triangles from each strip.

From **red plaid fabrics**, cut:
- 11 (5¾" x 44") strips.
  From these, cut 126 triangles, 8 half-triangles, and 8 half-triangles reversed.

From **green plaid fabrics**, cut:
- 13 (5¾" x 44") strips.
  From these, cut 154 triangles, 4 half-triangles, and 4 half-triangles reversed.

From **blue plaid fabrics**, cut:
- 12 (5¾" x 44") strips.
  From these, cut 134 triangles, 6 half-triangles, and 6 half-triangles reversed.

From **dark red print fabric**, cut:
- 9 (5"-wide) strips for outer border.

From **white print fabric**, cut:
- 9 (2"-wide) strips for inner border.

Quilt Top Assembly

1. Referring to photograph and *Quilt Top Assembly Diagram* on page 60, lay out triangles in 18 horizontal rows of 23 triangles each. Add 1 half-triangle at end of each row as shown. (Note that diagram shows bottom half of quilt. Turn diagram upside down to lay out top half.)

Rearrange triangles until satisfied with fabric placement. For center star, position darkest reds and blues as shown at center of Row 1.

2. Join triangles and half-triangles in each row.

3. Join rows as shown to complete bottom half of quilt. Repeat to make top half. Join halves, matching Row 1 to Row 1.

4. Join strips of white print fabric to make 2 (2" x 69½") borders and 2 (2" x 93½") borders. Sew shorter borders to top and bottom edges. Sew remaining borders to sides.

5. Join strips of red fabric to make 2 (5" x 72½") borders and 2 (5" x 102½") borders. Join these to quilt in same manner as for inner border.

Quilting and Finishing

1. Layer backing, batting, and quilt top. Quilt as desired. Quilt shown is machine-quilted in an all-over pattern.

2. Make 360" of bias or straight-grain binding. See page 31 for directions on making and applying binding.

gem from georgia

There's an advantage to being nearsighted. I take my glasses off when I'm shifting fabrics around to arrange a scrap quilt. This gives me a better perspective of colors because they seem farther away. If you aren't nearsighted, squinting will accomplish the same perspective.

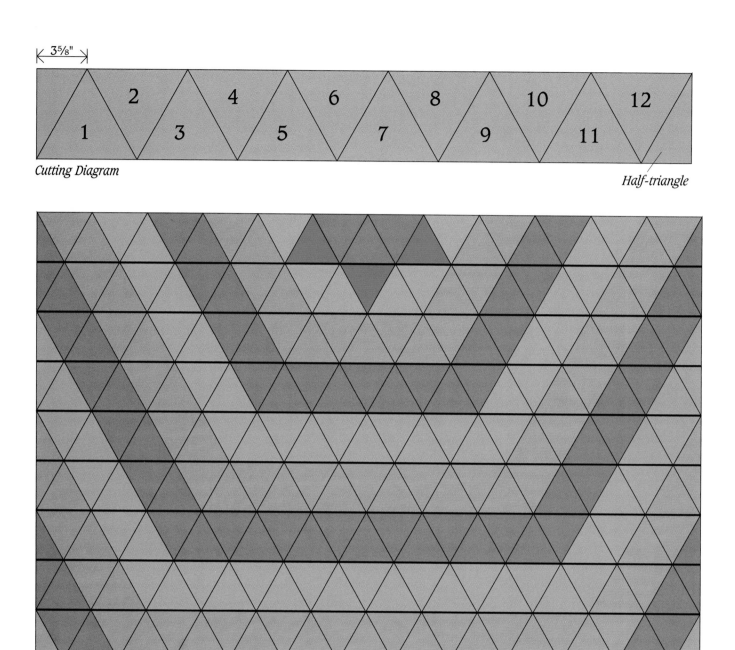

3⁵/₈"

2 4 6 8 10 12
1 3 5 7 9 11

Cutting Diagram

Half-triangle

Quilt Top Assembly Diagram

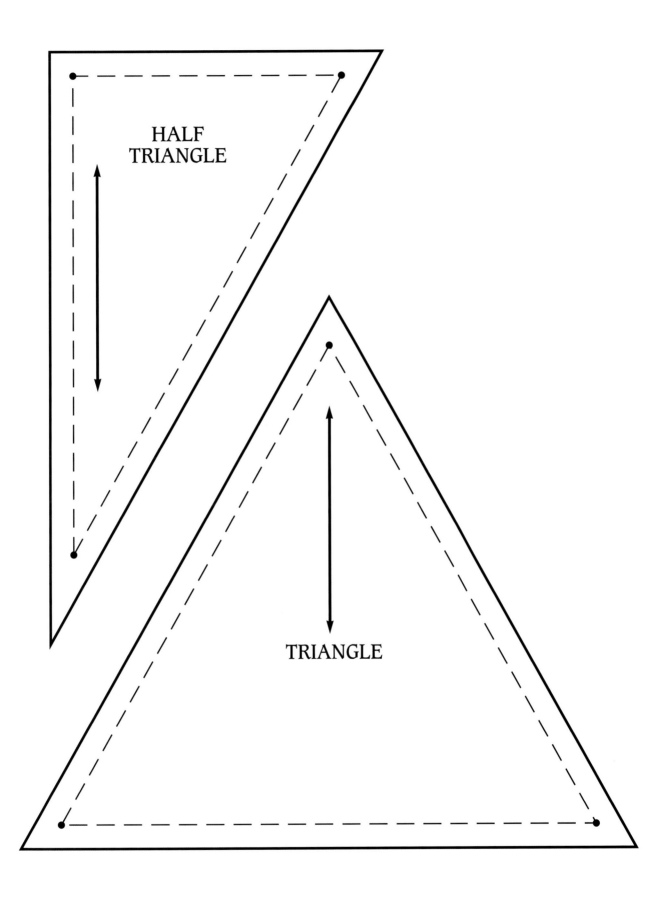

HALF
TRIANGLE

TRIANGLE

contemporary classics

Check & Double Check

Christmas Double Check
  Table Runner

Anvil & Stars

Fan Flowers

Cover Lovers' Cats

Brush Up

Diamond Flowers

Check & Double Check

Check & Double Check

Check out the mix of prints and woven plaids in this All-American quilt. Plaid "checks" interweave against a backdrop of vertical strips. The design was inspired by a scrap of wrapping paper and a glass panel I saw in a restaurant. These instructions call for eight prints and nine plaids. If you have lots of scraps, however, it's fun to mix more fabrics as I did in the quilt shown.

Finished Size
Blocks: 24 (8½" x 12") bar blocks
3 (4¼" x 12") half bar blocks
32 (8½" x 12") check blocks
4 (4¼" x 12") half check blocks
Quilt: 82¼" x 94"

Easy-Does-It Feature: Strip piecing

Materials
2¾ yards white fabric
1¼ yards navy fabric for middle border and binding
1 yard blue-on-white print fabric for outer border
½ yard red print fabric for inner border
½ yard *each* 9 red/navy plaids or ⅓ yard *each* 12 red/navy plaids (see Cutting Option at right)
⅜ yard *each* 4 red print fabrics
⅜ yard *each* 4 navy print fabrics
5½ yards of fabric for backing or 2¾ yards 90"-wide fabric

Cutting
Cut all strips cross-grain, except as noted.
From **white fabric,** cut:
9 (4¾" x 40") strips for bar blocks.
3 (6¼" x 42") strips.
From these, cut 17 (6¼") squares. Cut each square in quarters diagonally to get 4 triangles from each square, for a total of 68 C triangles.
9 (10¼") squares for D triangles.

From **navy solid fabric,** cut:
1 (30") square for binding.
8 (1½"-wide) strips for middle border.
From **blue-on-white fabric,** cut:
10 (3½"-wide) strips for outer border.
From **red print fabric,** cut:
8 (1½"-wide) strips for inner border.
From *each* **plaid fabric,** cut:
4 (3"-wide) bias strips as shown in *Diagram 1.* Stack strips in sets of 4. Referring to *Diagram 2,* trim each set to 23½" long. Measure 6⅞" from bottom and cut across layered strips at a right angle to get a set of 4 Bs; then measure 6⅞" on opposite side as shown and cut at a 45° angle to get 4 more Bs. Remainder of strip gives you 4 As. Repeat with remaining stacks to get 36 As and 72 Bs.
From *each* **print fabric,** cut:
1 (4¾"-wide) strip for bar blocks.
1 (10¼") square for D triangles.

Cutting Option
If you're cutting non-reversible fabrics, you'll want to make templates of patterns A and B on page 68. You'll get the most efficient use of yardage from 12 (⅓-yard) pieces of fabric. From each piece, cut 3 (10" x 14") rectangles.
Referring to *Diagram 3,* cut 1 A and 2 Bs from each piece.

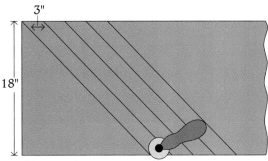

Diagram 1

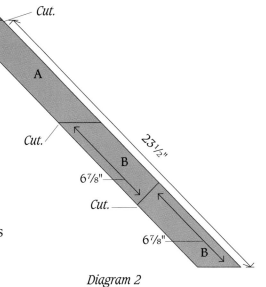

Diagram 2

Diagram 3

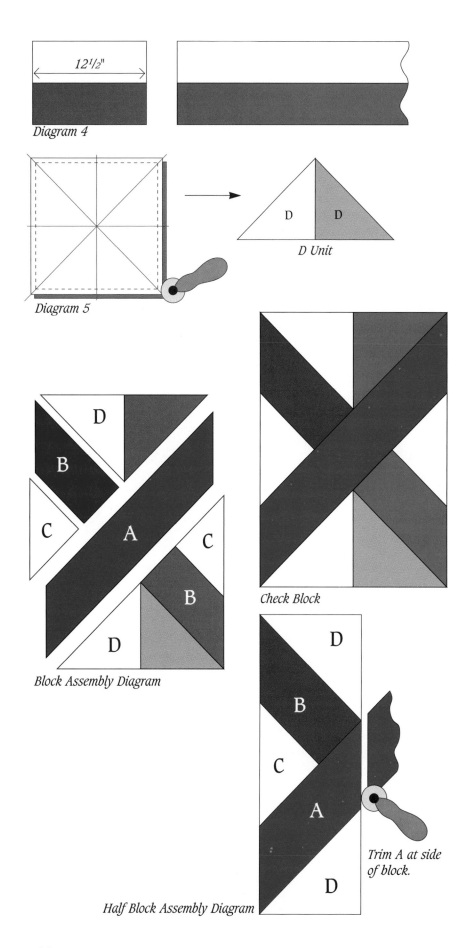

Diagram 4

Diagram 5

D Unit

Block Assembly Diagram

Check Block

Trim A at side of block.

Half Block Assembly Diagram

Piecing Bar Blocks

1. With right sides facing, join a 4¾"-wide white strip to 1 print strip along 1 long edge. Make 8 strip sets. Press seam allowances toward print fabrics.

2. Referring to *Diagram 4,* cut 3 (12½"-long) segments from each strip set, for a total of 24 segments. Each segment is 1 bar block.

3. From remaining white strip, cut 3 (4¾" x 12½") segments for half blocks.

Piecing Check Blocks

1. With right sides facing, match a 10¼" white square with a 10¼" square of print fabric. Referring to *Diagram 5,* stitch a ¼" seam around all sides of square. Cut stitched square into 8 D triangle units as shown. Press seam allowances toward white fabric. Repeat with remaining 10¼" squares to get 32 red D units and 32 navy D units.

2. Cut remaining 10¼" white square in same manner to get 8 D triangles. Set these aside for half blocks.

3. Now that all units are prepared, take time out to play with different fabric arrangements before assembling check blocks. Referring to *Block Assembly Diagram,* photograph, and *Quilt Top Assembly Diagram,* lay out bar blocks in rows; then arrange units for check blocks. Position units for half blocks at right side, using 1 A, 1 B, 1 C, and 2 Ds for each half check block. (Piece A will be trimmed after half block is joined.) Rearrange prints and plaids until satisfied with placement. Discard 4 extra Bs.

4. To assemble block, join 1 B and 1 C; then join B-C unit to D unit as shown in *Block Assembly Diagram.* Press seam allowance away from B. Repeat to make another B-C-D unit. Then join B-C-D units to A; press these seam allowances toward A. Make 32 check blocks.

5. Refer to *Half Block Assembly Diagram* to make 4 half blocks. Trim A even with Ds at right side of each block.

Quilt Top Assembly

1. Referring to *Quilt Top Assembly Diagram,* lay out assembled blocks and half blocks in 9 vertical rows, alternating check blocks and bar blocks as shown. Join blocks in each row. Join rows.

2. Join red border strips to make 2 (1½" x 74¾") borders and 2 (1½" x 84½") borders. Sew longer borders to quilt sides; then sew shorter borders to top and bottom edges of quilt.

3. For middle border, join strips of navy solid fabric to make 2 (1½" x 76¾") borders and 2 (1½" x 86½") borders. Join these to quilt top in same manner as for inner border.

4. For outer border, join strips of blue-on-white fabric to make 2 (3½" x 82¾") borders and 2 (3½" x 88½") borders. Join borders to quilt; then miter corners.

Quilting and Finishing

1. Make a stencil for star quilting design (see page 69). Mark stars on D units and bar blocks as shown in *Quilting Diagram.* Add a 2" square between stars in center of each bar block.

2. Layer backing, batting, and quilt top. Outline-quilt checks; then quilt marked designs. (To make star stand out, I used red or blue quilting thread on white fabric and white thread on colored side of bars.) Quilt borders as desired.

3. Make 360" of bias or straight-grain binding. See page 31 for directions on making and applying binding.

Quilt Top Assembly Diagram

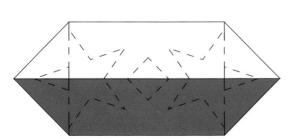

Quilting Diagram

gem from georgia

For a different look, shorten the bar blocks between the check rows to 10" or less.

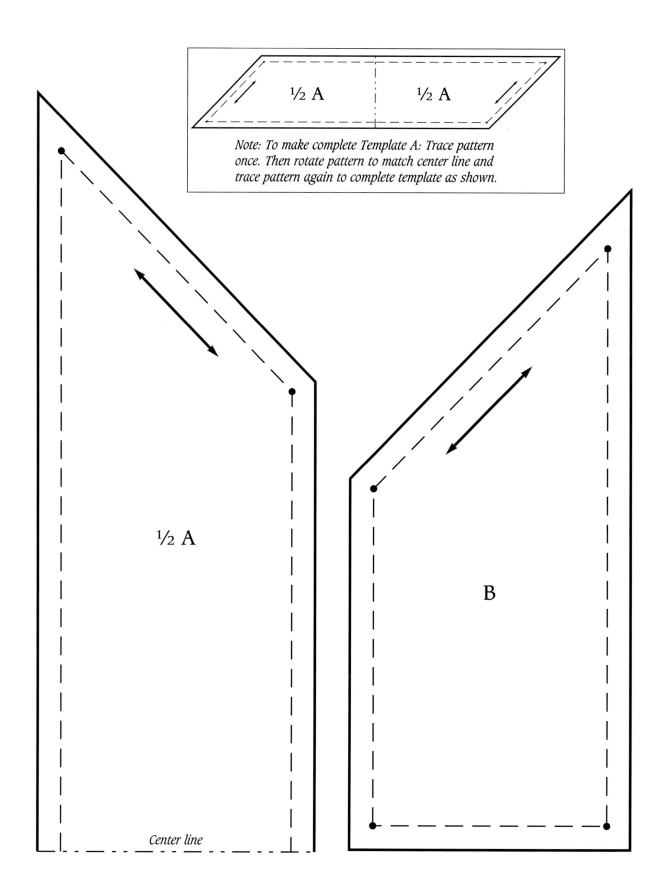

½ A   ½ A

Note: To make complete Template A: Trace pattern once. Then rotate pattern to match center line and trace pattern again to complete template as shown.

½ A

Center line

B

Star Quilting Design

Christmas Double Check Table Runner

Because the festive colors and prints of Christmas are such a pleasure to work with, I just love to make things for seasonal decorating. This table runner is a quick project to make for your holiday decorating. It's another version of my check block, shown on page 64, interpreted in just two contrasting fabrics that are accented with Christmas print fabrics.

Finished Size
Blocks: 8 (8½" x 12") blocks
Table Runner: 18" x 68"

Easy-Does-It Feature: Strip piecing

Materials
½ yard *each* 2 contrasting plaid fabrics
⅝ yard white fabric or muslin
⅜ yard *each* 2 coordinating Christmas prints
1 yard backing fabric

Cutting
Cut all strips cross-grain.
From *each* **plaid fabric,** cut:
4 As and 8 Bs. See instructions on page 65 for cutting options, instructions, and diagrams.
6 (4") squares for prairie points.

From **white fabric,** cut:
2 (4¾" x 28") strips for border.
2 (10¼") squares for D triangles.
4 (6¼") squares.
Cut each square in quarters diagonally to get 4 triangles from each square, for a total of 16 C triangles.
From *each* **print fabric,** cut:
1 (4¾" x 28") strip for border.
1 (10¼") square for D triangles.

Piecing Check Blocks
1. With right sides facing, match a 10¼" white square with a 10¼" square of print fabric. Referring to *Diagram 1,* stitch a ¼" seam around all sides of square. Cut stitched square into 8 D triangle units as shown. Press seam allowances toward white fabric. Repeat with remaining 10¼" squares to get 8 more D units.
2. Following block instructions on page 66, make 8 check blocks.

Table Runner Assembly
1. Join 1 (4¾" x 28") strip of white fabric to each matching strip of print fabric to make 2 strip sets. Press seam allowances toward print fabric. Referring to *Diagram 2,* cut 8 (3½"-wide) segments from each strip set to get 16 border segments.

2. Referring to *Diagram 3* and photograph, join border segments to top and bottom of each block, matching print fabrics as shown.

3. Referring to photograph, join blocks in a row.

Finishing

1. Referring to *Diagram 4,* fold each 4" square as shown to make 12 prairie points. With right sides facing and raw edges aligned, pin 6 prairie points at each end of runner, alternating fabrics as shown in photograph. Fit each prairie point into fold of adjacent prairie point to space them evenly along edge of runner.

2. Piece an 18½" x 68½" backing. With right sides facing, sew backing to runner around all sides, leaving a 5" opening in 1 side.

3. Turn right side out through opening and press. Hand-stitch opening closed.

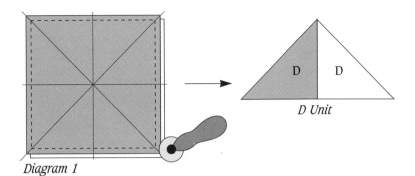

D Unit

Diagram 1

3½"

Diagram 2

Diagram 3

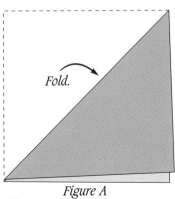

Fold.

Fold.

Figure A

Figure B

Diagram 4

Anvil & Stars

72

Anvil & Stars

Four Anvil blocks and nine stars combine in a clever interchange. Keitha Kierbow made this quilt for her husband, John. He helped to select fabrics that reflect the colors of tempered and heated metal. Keitha expanded on the blacksmith theme by adding hammer and tong quilting motifs.

Finished Size
Blocks: 4 (16") Anvil blocks
Quilt: 70" x 70"

Easy-Does-It Feature: 4-in-1
Flying Geese

Materials
4¼ yards red print fabric
(includes backing and mock binding)
2 yards black solid or miniprint fabric
1½ yards gold solid fabric
1 yard dark yellow print fabric
½ yard gray print fabric
¼ yard *each* brown, violet, blue, yellow, dark gold, and gold-on-white print fabrics for Flying Geese

Cutting
Cut all strips cross-grain except borders as indicated. Make templates for patterns A and B on page 77.
From **red fabric**, cut:
2 (36½" x 72½") pieces for backing.
36 Bs and 36 Bs reversed.
6 (5¼") squares for Flying Geese.
From **black fabric**, cut:
2 (3½" x 70½") lengthwise strips and 2 (3½" x 64½") lengthwise strips for outer border.
2 (2½" x 56½") lengthwise strips and 2 (2½" x 52½") lengthwise strips for inner border.
3 (9¾") squares for triangle-square units.
6 (5¼") squares for Flying Geese.

From **gold solid fabric**, cut:
52 (4½") squares.
4 (9¾") squares for triangle-square units.
6 (5¾") squares for Flying Geese.
12 As.
From **dark yellow print fabric**, cut:
33 (4½") squares.
6 (5¾") squares for Flying Geese.
24 As.
From **gray print fabric**, cut:
3 (9¾") squares for triangle-square units.
8 (4½") squares.
From each of **brown, violet, and blue fabrics**, cut:
6 (5¼") squares.
From each of **yellow, dark gold, and gold-on-white print fabrics**, cut:
6 (5¾") squares.

Making Anvil Blocks
1. For triangle-squares, sort 9¾" squares to get 1 gray/black pair, 2 gray/gold pairs, and 2 gold/black pairs.
2. For 1 gold/gray pair, mark a grid on wrong side of gold square, as shown in *Diagram 1, Figure A*. Stitch on both sides of diagonal lines as shown in *Figure B*; then cut on all drawn lines to get 8 triangle-squares. Repeat with remaining squares to get 8 gray/black squares, 16 gray/gold squares, and 16 gold/black squares. Stagger allowances. Trim dog-ears.
3. For 1 block, lay out triangle-squares with 4½" gray and gold squares, as shown in *Anvil Block Assembly Diagram*.
4. Join units into 4 four-patches as shown, staggering seam allowances.
5. Join adjacent four-patches; then join halves to complete block.
6. Make 4 Anvil blocks.

Diagram 1

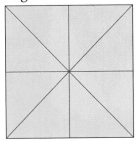

Figure A

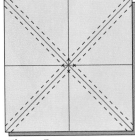

Figure B

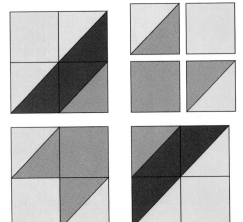

Anvil Block Assembly Diagram

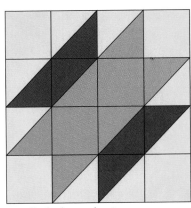

Anvil Block—Make 4.

Diagram 2

Figure A—Make 24.

Figure B—Make 12.

Diagram 3—Make 12.

Quilt Top Assembly

1. Referring to *Diagram 2,* sew 1 B and 1 B reversed to sides of each A. Press seam allowances toward Bs. Trim dog-ears.

2. Referring to *Diagram 3,* join 2 red/dark yellow star points with dark yellow squares to make 1 sashing unit. Press seam allowances toward squares. Make 12 sashing units.

3. Join 4 (4½") gold squares in a row. Press seam allowances toward ends of row. Make 8 (4-square) rows.

4. Referring to *Quilt Top Assembly Diagram,* join units in horizontal rows, making 5 sashing rows and 2 block rows as shown. Join rows.

5. Sew 2½" x 52½" black borders to top and bottom edges of quilt top. Press seam allowances toward borders. Sew 2½" x 56½" black borders to quilt sides.

Piecing Flying Geese Border

See optional 4-in-1 piecing method on page 76.

1. The 6 (5¼") squares each of red, black, brown, violet, and blue fabrics are for geese. Cut each square as shown in *Diagram 4* to get 24 triangles of each fabric.

2. The 6 (5¾") squares each of gold, dark yellow, yellow, dark gold, and gold-on-white fabrics are for geese backgrounds. Cut each square as shown in *Diagram 5* to get 48 triangles of each fabric.

3. Referring to *Flying Geese Diagram,* stitch 1 gold triangle to 1 black "goose." Press seam allowance toward gold triangle; then add another gold triangle to opposite side of goose. In this manner, make 24 geese of each fabric combination— black/gold, blue/dark yellow,

violet/yellow, brown/gold-on-white, and red/dark gold.

4. Set red/dark gold geese aside. Join remaining geese in groups of 4 as shown in *Flying Geese Diagram.* Make 24 Flying Geese units.

5. Referring to photograph, lay out 6 Flying Geese units in a row with all brown geese pointing toward center of row. Slip red geese between units except at center where brown geese meet. Join units to make 1 border. Make 4 borders in this manner.

6. Join 1 border to top edge of quilt. Press seam allowance toward black border. Repeat for bottom border.

7. Referring to *Border Corner Diagram,* join 2 red/dark gold geese to make a corner block. Make 4 corner blocks.

8. Join corner blocks to both ends of each remaining border. Sew borders to quilt sides.

9. Sew 3½" x 64½" black borders to top and bottom edges of quilt top. Press seam allowances toward borders. Sew 3½" x 70½" black borders to quilt sides.

Quilting and Finishing

1. Piece backing to make a 72½" square.

2. Layer backing, batting, and quilt top. Backing should be 1¼" larger than quilt top on all sides. Quilt as desired.

3. Trim batting even with quilt top.

4. To make mock binding, press under ¼" on each side of backing. At top edge, fold backing over to front of quilt top, making a 1"-wide band. Quilt hemmed edge in place through all layers. Repeat at bottom edge. Finish sides in same manner.

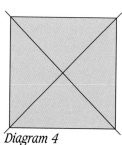

Diagram 4

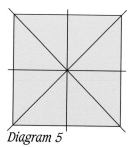

Diagram 5

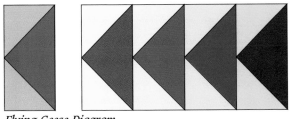

Flying Geese Diagram

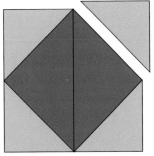

Border Corner Diagram

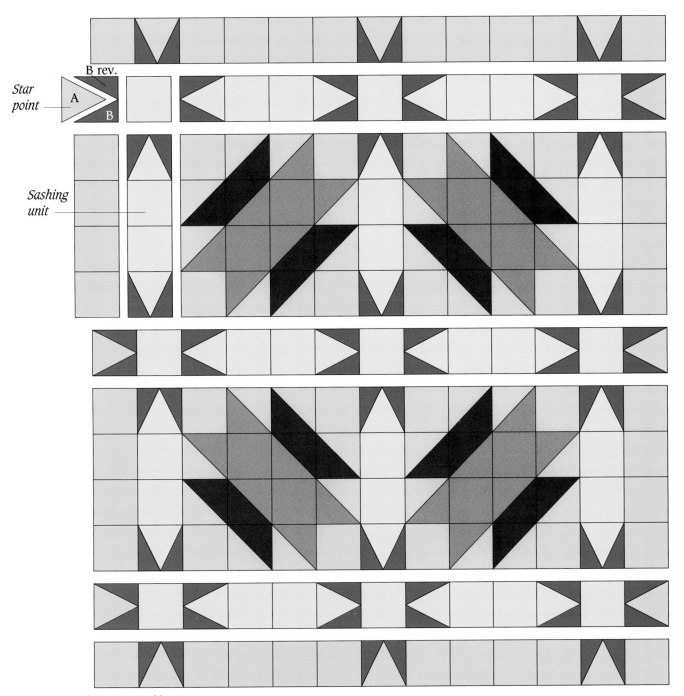

Star point

B rev.

A

B

Sashing unit

Quilt Top Assembly Diagram

Quick Piecing 4-in-1 Flying Geese

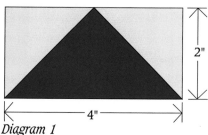

Diagram 1

This is a fast and nifty way to make 4 Flying Geese units from 2 precut squares. I learned this wonderful technique from my English friend Pauline Adams.

1. To make 4 Flying Geese, you need 1 square for geese and 1 square for background. The geese square is always 1¼" larger than the base of the finished geese triangle. The background square is always twice the finished leg of the sky triangle plus 1¾". For *Anvil & Stars,* each Flying Geese unit is a finished size of 2" x 4" *(Diagram 1)*. So we start with a geese square of 5¼" (4" + 1¼") and a background square of 5¾" ([2" x 2"] + 1¾").

2. On wrong side of background square, draw diagonal lines in both directions *(Diagram 2, Figure A)*. Then cut square in quarters as indicated by red lines *(Figure B)* to get 4 (2⅞") square units *(Figure C)*.

3. On each 2⅞" square, trim a ⅜" triangle from 1 corner *(Diagram 3)*.

4. With right sides facing, position 2 small squares at opposite corners of geese square *(Diagram 4)*. Stitch ¼" on both sides of diagonal lines.

5. Finger-press stitched squares out of the way as shown. Then pin a third small square unit in open corner and stitch as before *(Diagram 5)*. Take care not to stitch over previously sewn squares.

6. Repeat Step 5 with last small square unit *(Diagram 6)*, again being careful not to stitch over previous squares.

7. Cut on pencil lines between stitching to get 4 Flying Geese units *(Diagram 7)*. Press seam allowances toward background triangles. Trim dog-ears.

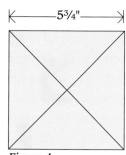

Figure A

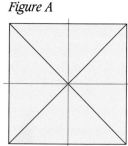

Figure B

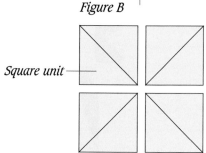

Square unit

Diagram 2   *Figure C*

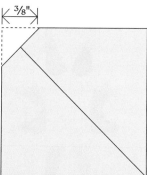

Diagram 3

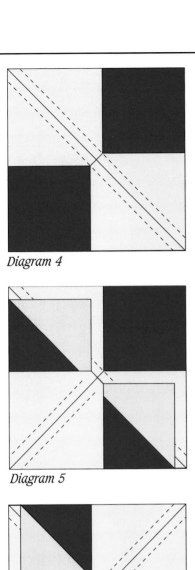

Diagram 4

Diagram 5

Diagram 6

Diagram 7

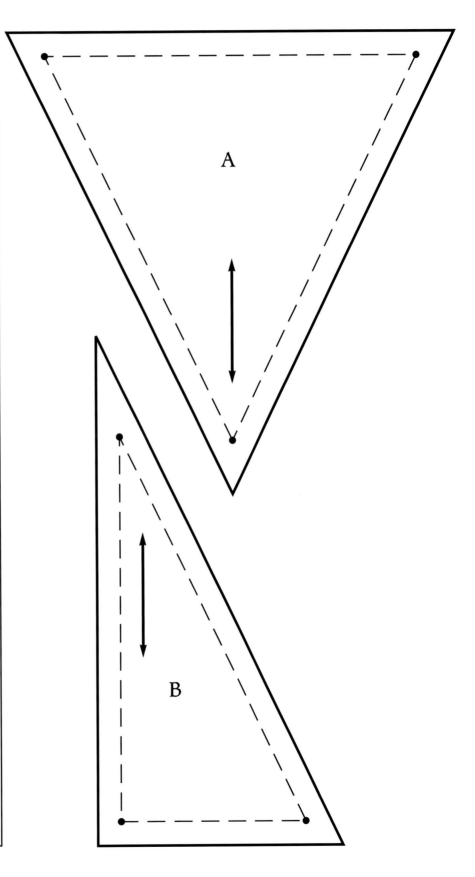

A

B

Fan Flowers

Fan Flowers

This quilt can be made traditionally, but I did it all by machine and quilted it in sections that were then joined with my lap-quilting technique. Borders aren't joined as separate units. Instead, a section of each of the outside blocks becomes the border when all the blocks are joined.

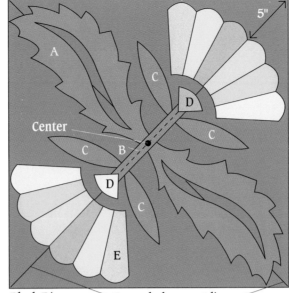

Block Diagram — Creased placement lines

Finished Size
Quilt: 81½" x 102"

Easy-Does-It Feature: Lap quilting

Materials
7¾ yards royal blue fabric (includes binding)
1¾ yards green print fabric
¼ yard *each* 6 pastel print fabrics
6¾ yards fabric for backing
Spray sizing (optional)

Cutting
Make templates for patterns A, B, C, D, E, and F on pages 82 and 83, following directions on patterns A and F to make full-size patterns.

From **royal blue fabric,** cut:
2 (21") squares (for center), 6 (21" x 31") rectangles (for sides), and 4 (31") squares (for corners) for block backgrounds.

From **green fabric,** cut:
12 As and 12 As reversed (large leaf).
12 Bs (stem).
56 Cs (small leaf).
28 Fs (border vine).
Note: If centers are removed from A leaves very carefully, you can use those pieces for Fs. However, yardage allows for separate cutting.

From **assorted pastel fabrics,** cut:
56 Cs (small leaf).
28 Ds (fan base).
156 Es (fan petal).

From **backing fabric,** cut:
2 (21") squares, 6 (21" x 31") rectangles, and 4 (31") squares.

Appliquéing Blocks
1. For each fan, select 1 E of each pastel print. Referring to *Block Diagram,* join 6 E pieces side by side to make 1 fan. Turn under seam allowance on all sides of completed unit and press or baste. Make 24 fans for blocks. For border corners, join 3 E pieces to make each of 4 half fans.

2. Referring to *Diagram 1,* use chalk to mark 10¼" border on 2 sides of each 31" square of blue fabric and 1 short side of each 21" x 31" piece.

3. Referring to *Diagram 2,* fold and press block areas to mark diagonal placement lines on all 10 pieces. Press placement lines on 21" squares in same manner.

4. Press appliqué pieces with spray sizing to give them stability and crispness for appliqué.

5. Using diagonal placement lines as a guide, center and pin a stem (B) on 1 block as shown in *Diagram 2.* Referring to *Block Diagram,* position 2 A leaves, 2 D bases, and 4 C leaves as shown and pin. Pin 2 fans at corners, aligning center seams with placement line 5" from corner of block. Use flat-headed pins or basting to secure pieces in place. (*Hint:* To place pieces precisely every time, make a full-size window template. Trace complete design on a 20½" square of paper and cut out shapes. Place this on top of each block as a placement guide to check position of appliqués.)

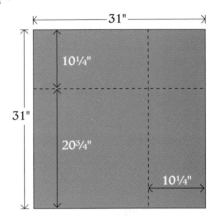

Diagram 1

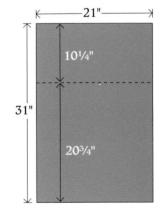

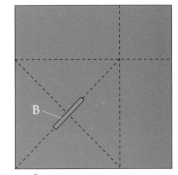

Diagram 2

6. Set machine as desired for appliqué.

7. Matching top and bobbin threads to appliqué fabric, begin appliqué by stitching long sides of stem. Place a sheet of thin paper (unprinted newsprint is best) under background fabric to act as a stabilizer. If necessary, use a stiletto or seam ripper to keep figures in place when stitching. Stitch large and small leaves; then change to a light-colored thread to stitch base and fans.

8. Appliqué 12 blocks in this manner. Refer to *Quilt Top Assembly Diagram* to verify direction of stem for each block. Red lines indicate block division.

9. Repeat to appliqué borders.

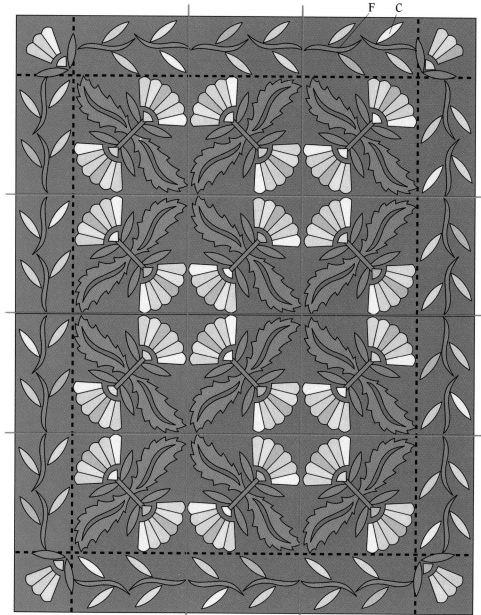

Quilt Top Assembly Diagram

Lap Quilting and Finishing

1. Cut a batting piece to match each piece of backing fabric. Pin or baste batting to wrong side of backing.

2. Quilt blocks by hand or machine as desired. I used my machine's decorative stitches to echo leaf and petal shapes. Randomly placed butterflies fill in the background, which is stitched in a meandering pattern around the fans. (Butterfly patterns are on next page.) Leave at least ½" unquilted at all inside edges.

3. When quilting is complete, trim blocks so all sides are even. Referring to *Quilt Top Assembly Diagram,* lay out blocks in 4 horizontal rows of 3 blocks each.

4. Select 2 adjacent blocks. Stack blocks with right sides facing. Align blocks along edge to be sewn. On top block of pair, pin batting and backing away from seam as shown in *Diagram 3.* On bottom block, pin backing only away from seam. Pin blocks together at corners and center of seam to be sewn. Machine-stitch ¼" seam through 3 layers as shown. Join remaining block in row in same manner. Join blocks to make 4 rows.

5. For each row, finger-press seam allowances in 1 direction, alternating direction from row to row. Unpin batting and backings.

6. Lay 1 row flat with backing side up. Trim batting so adjacent pieces butt without overlap. At each seam, smooth backing flat so edges overlap. On top layer of backing fabric, turn under ¼" hem. Slipstitch hemmed edge to opposite backing fabric, taking care that stitches do not go through to front side. Complete backing seams on all 4 rows.

7. Join rows in same manner, pinning backings and batting away from seam before stitching *(Diagram 4).* Hand-sew backing seams as before.

8. From remaining blue fabric, make 376" of bias or straight-grain binding. See page 31 for directions on making and applying binding.

80

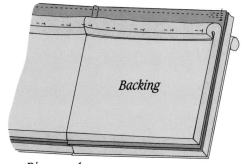

Batting

Backing

Diagram 3

Backing

Diagram 4

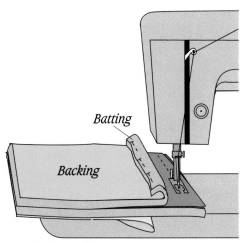

Butterfly Quilting Designs

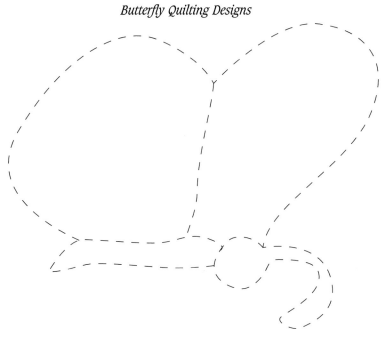

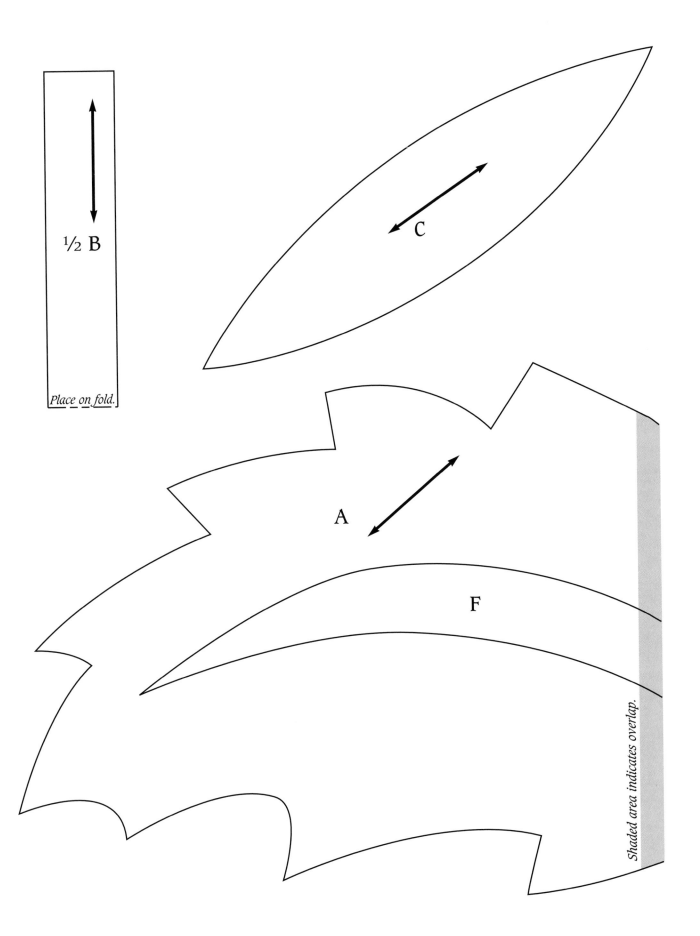

½ B

Place on fold.

C

A

F

Shaded area indicates overlap.

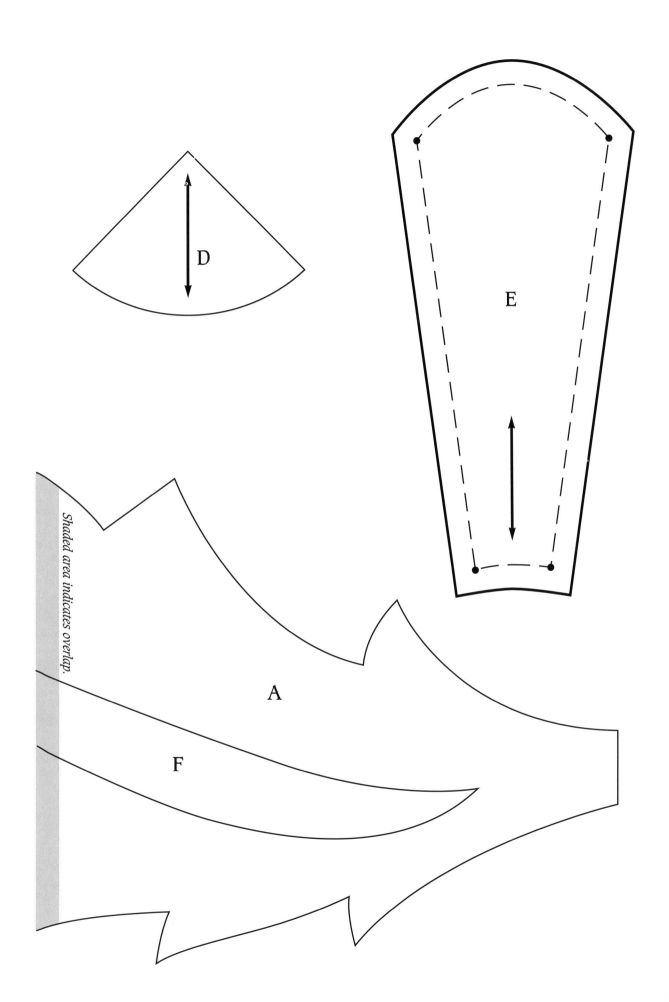

D

E

Shaded area indicates overlap.

A

F

Cover Lovers' Cats

Cover Lovers' Cats

In this original design, 20 contented kitties snuggle into bright baskets. Note how the cats' tails curl all the way around to take the place of a basket handle. Finding fabrics to mimic the fur of our favorite felines was a challenge for the Cover Lovers, a group that's been quilting together for more than 10 years. We're friends and we all have cats, so we made this quilt a collective project.

Finished Size
Blocks: 20 (14") blocks
Quilt: 82" x 100"

Easy-Does-It Feature: Personalizing blocks with embellishment

Materials
3¾ yards plaid fabric for sashing and borders
3 yards light-colored background fabric*
½ yard red solid fabric for middle border
20 (11" x 15") assorted print fabrics for cats
20 (8" x 15") assorted solid fabrics for baskets
Assorted scraps for eyes, ears, and noses
1 yard blue solid fabric for binding
6 yards fabric for backing or 3 yards 90"-wide fabric
Coordinating embroidery floss for cat details
*Note: Quilt shown has 2 cats stitched on dark fabric for contrast. If you vary backgrounds in this manner, adjust yardage accordingly.

Cutting
Cut all strips cross-grain except plaid borders as indicated. Make templates for patterns A, B, C, D, and E on pages 86–89. Trace A in 1 piece, joining halves as indicated on patterns.
From **background fabric**, cut:
  20 (14½") squares for cat backgrounds.
From **print and scrap fabrics**, cut:
  20 As (cat).
  20 Cs (nose).
  20 Ds (ears) and 20 Ds reversed.
  20 Es (eyes) and 20 Es reversed.
From **solid fabrics**, cut:
  20 Bs (basket).
From **solid red fabric**, cut:
  8 (1½"-wide) strips for middle border.
From **plaid fabric**, cut:
  1 (32") square.
    From this, make 328" of 2½"-wide continuous bias. From bias, cut 2 (90½"-long) strips and 2 (74½"-long) strips for inner border.
  2 (4½" x 100½") lengthwise strips and 2 (4½" x 82½") lengthwise strips for outer border.
  3 (4½" x 86½") lengthwise strips for vertical sashing.
  16 (4½" x 14½") strips for horizontal sashing.

Making Blocks
1. With right sides facing, machine-stitch bottom of 1 cat (A) to top of its basket (B). Clip seam allowance as necessary. Press seam allowances toward cat. Turn and press under all seam allowances except bottom edge of basket.

2. With right sides up, align bottom of basket with background square. Top of tail should be ½" from top raw edge of background square. Appliqué cat body, tail, and basket to background. When appliqué is complete, trim background from under appliqué, leaving a ¼" seam allowance.

3. Appliqué ears, eyes, and nose. Use 3 strands of floss to outline-stitch whiskers, mouth, tail detail, and hind leg, indicated by broken lines on pattern. (See *Stitch Diagram.*) Some Cover Lovers added buttons or embroidery lines to give dimension to eyes. Some noses are triangular buttons or embroidered instead of appliquéd.

4. Repeat steps 1–3 to make 20 blocks.

Stitch Diagram

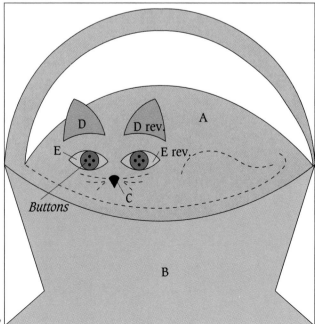

Block Diagram

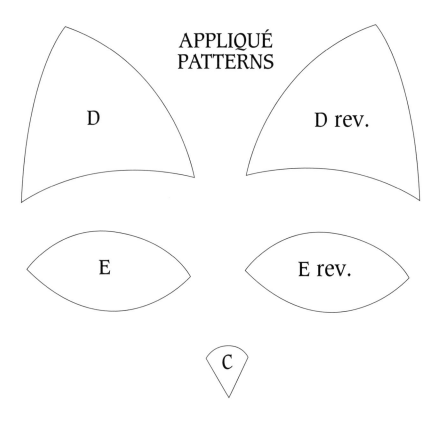

APPLIQUÉ PATTERNS

D

D rev.

E

E rev.

C

5. To personalize each block, I stitched each cat's name at the bottom of its basket. Among my favorites are my parents' North Carolina cats, "Tar" and "Heel." And then there's my friend Audrey's "Indigo Jones," for whom she naturally used hand-dyed fabric. Be creative with embroidery, quilting, buttons, bows—anything!—to personalize your cats as desired.

Quilt Top Assembly

1. Referring to photograph, arrange blocks in 4 vertical rows of 5 blocks each. Join blocks in each row with horizontal sashing strip between blocks. Press seam allowances toward sashing strips.

2. Join rows with vertical sashing strips between rows as shown. Press seam allowances toward sashing strips.

3. For middle border, join red strips to make 2 (74½"-long) borders and 2 (92½"-long) borders.

4. Matching centers, join 1 (90½"-long) bias strip to 1 (92½"-long) red strip. Add 1 (100½"-long) plaid border to opposite side of red strip in same manner. Sew combined border unit to 1 side edge of quilt, keeping border against feed dogs to protect bias edge from stretching. Repeat for opposite side.

5. Join remaining border strips in sets in same manner, always matching centers. Join borders to top and bottom edges of quilt top. Miter border corners.

Quilting and Finishing

1. Layer backing fabric, batting, and quilt top. Quilt as desired. I used ½"-wide masking tape as a guide to quilt a woven cross-hatching in each basket. Appliqué is outline-quilted.

2. From blue fabric, make 370" of bias or straight-grain binding. See page 31 for directions on making and applying binding.

gem from georgia

My cat, Pee Wee, likes to eat cotton batting, so I'm careful to keep it where he can't get to it. Be sure to store all supplies where they are safely out of reach of pets and small children.

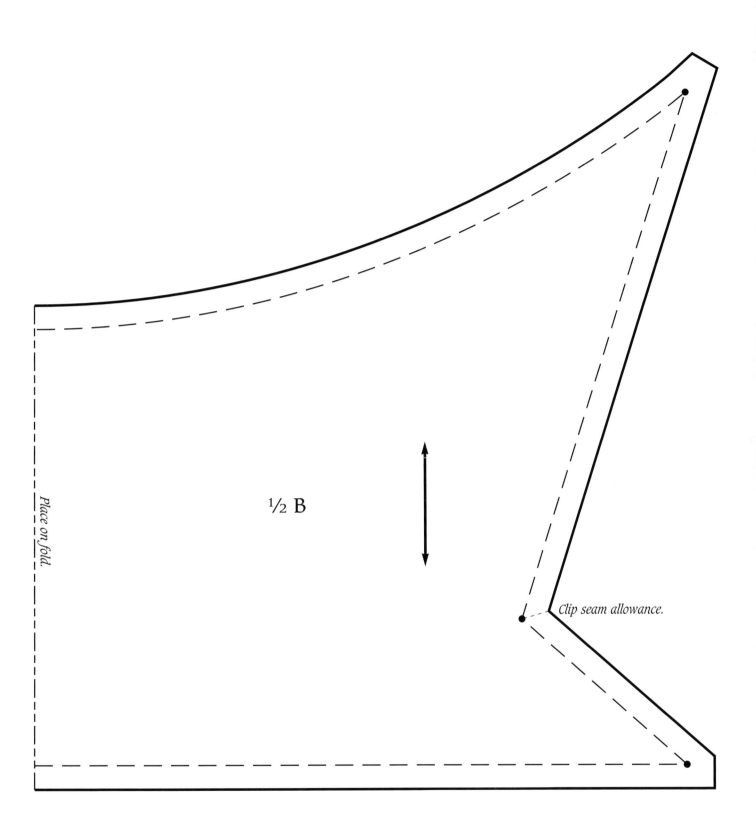

½ B

Place on fold.

Clip seam allowance.

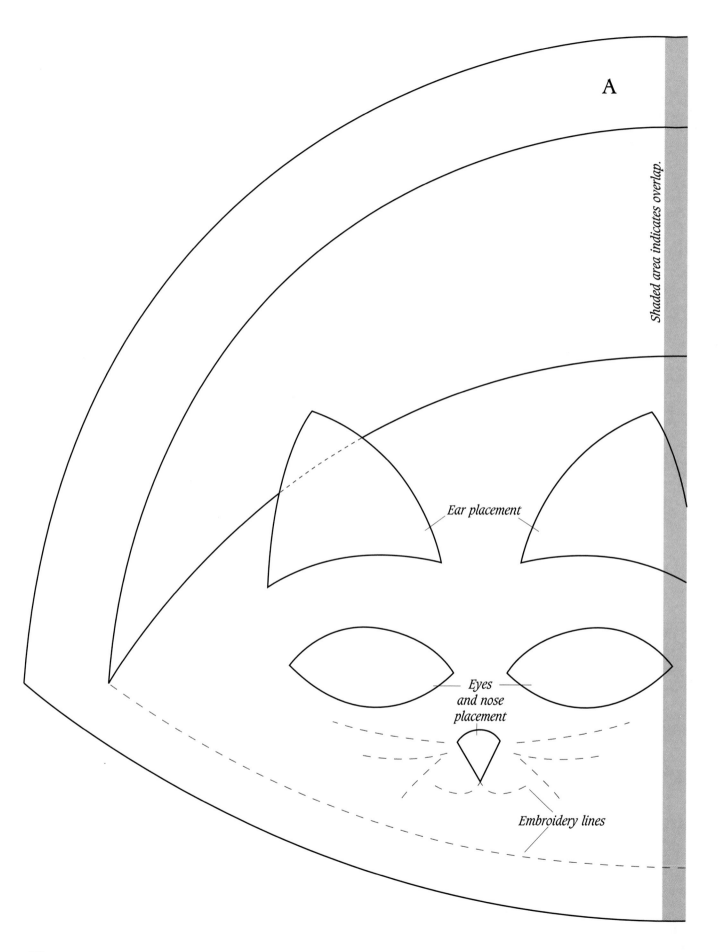

A

Ear placement

Eyes
and nose
placement

Embroidery lines

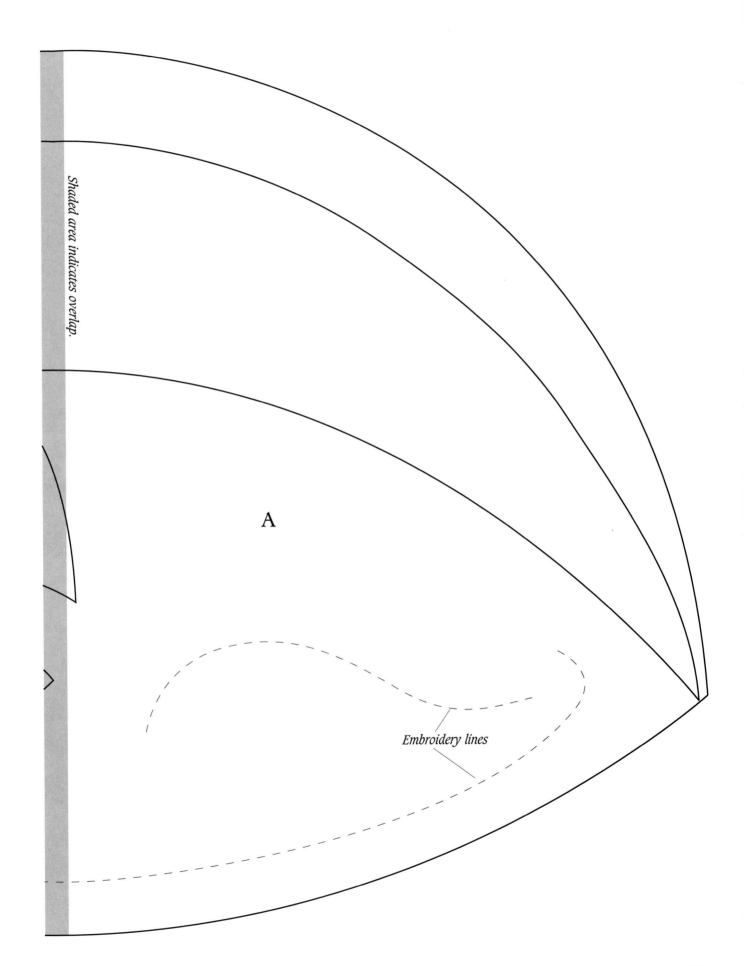

Shaded area indicates overlap.

A

Embroidery lines

89

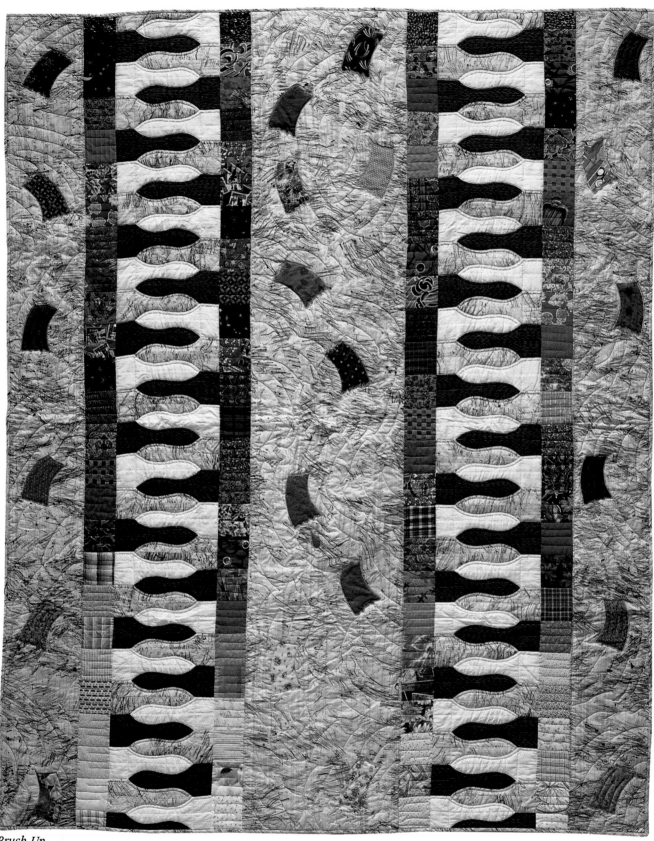

Brush Up

Brush Up

Two bands of paintbrushes march up and down this quilt in precision patchwork. The bristles represent the full range of the color wheel on both sides of each band. The paint swipes appliquéd on the connecting panels make lively accents.

Finished Size
Blocks: 50 (4" x 13½") blocks
Quilt: 83" x 100"

Easy-Does-It Feature: All-in-one machine appliqué and quilting

Materials
5 yards gray marbled fabric (includes binding)
1⅜ yards white fabric
1⅜ yards black fabric
102 (4½") assorted squares for brush bristles
22 (6½") assorted squares for paint swipes
6 yards fabric for backing or 3 yards 90"-wide fabric

Cutting
From freezer paper, make templates for patterns B, B reversed, and C on page 92.
From **gray fabric,** cut:
   1 (20½" x 100½") lengthwise strip for center panel.
   2 (10½" x 100½") lengthwise strips for side panels.
   33 As and 33 As reversed.
From **white fabric,** cut:
   34 As and 34 As reversed.
From **black fabric,** cut:
   33 As and 33 As reversed.

Piecing Paintbrush Panels
1. Referring to *Block Assembly Diagrams,* join A pieces in pairs as shown; then join pairs to complete blocks.

2. For left paintbrush panel, join blocks in 1-2-3 order, working from the top down (see photograph). For right panel, join reversed blocks in same order. Press seam allowances toward top of panels.

3. For paintbrush bristles, sort 4½" squares into 4 vertical rows. Starting with darkest prints at top, arrange colors from green to blue-green, blue, blue-violet, red-violet, red, rust, orange, and yellow. Arrange 2 rows of 26 squares each and 2 rows of 25 squares each, balancing colors. Join squares in each row. Press seam allowances toward bottom of row.

4. Matching seam lines, join a 26-square row to left edge of left paintbrush panel; then trim squares at top and bottom of row even with raw edge of panel. Join a 25-square row to right edge of panel. Join rows to right paintbrush panel in same manner, sewing 26-square row to right edge of panel and 25-square row to left edge.

Block Assembly Diagrams

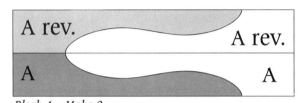
Block 1—Make 9.

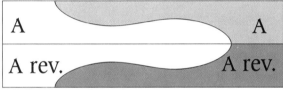
Block 1 Reversed—Make 9.

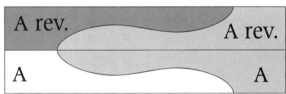
Block 2—Make 8.

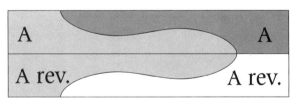
Block 2 Reversed—Make 8.

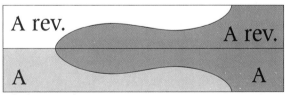
Block 3—Make 8.

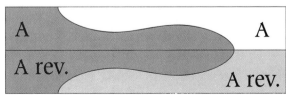
Block 3 Reversed—Make 8.

Appliquéing Side and Center Panels

1. To make paint swipes, arrange 6½" rectangles right side up on right side of center and side panels (see photograph). Pin 10 rectangles in place on center panel and 6 rectangles on each side panel.

2. Press freezer-paper Template B (swipe) onto 1 rectangle, aligning grain line with fabric grain. Topstitch around template. Remove freezer paper and trim print fabric up to stitching line. Repeat for each paint swipe. Use Template C to add desired drips in same manner.

Quilt Top Assembly

1. Referring to photograph, join paintbrush panels to each side of center panel. Add side panels.

2. Layer backing fabric, batting, and quilt top. Baste.

Roll up quilt sides to handle quilt in sewing machine. You might want to use a small hoop to stabilize area of quilt on which you are working.

3. With machine set to make a narrow zigzag, stitch through all layers around paint swipes. At bottom of each swipe, drop feed dogs and lengthen stitches to create illusion of random brush strokes (see photo below). Machine-stitch drips in same manner.

Quilting and Finishing

1. Outline-quilt brushes by hand or machine. Quilt parallel lines, 1" apart, in each print square for bristles. Add echo quilting around swipes and drips.

2. From remaining gray fabric, make 372" of bias or straight-grain binding. See page 31 for directions on making and applying binding.

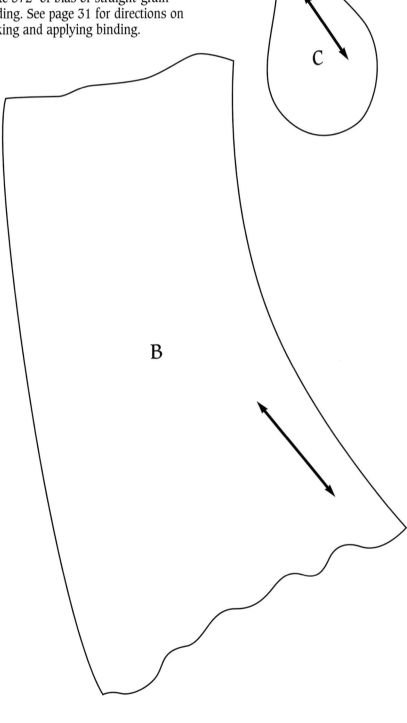

C

B

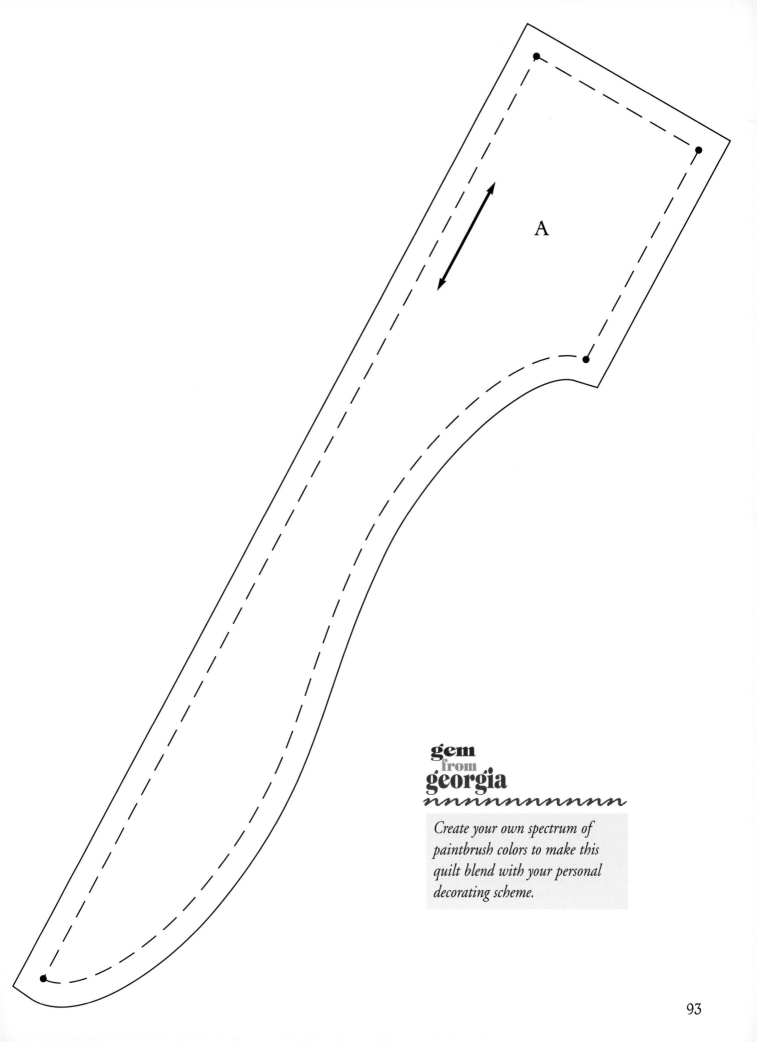

A

gem
from
georgia

Create your own spectrum of paintbrush colors to make this quilt blend with your personal decorating scheme.

93

Diamond Flowers

Diamond Flowers

Solid-colored fabrics sparkle against a black background in this dynamic design based on 60° diamonds. Rotary-cut and strip-pieced Log Cabin style, the design is created by alternating two pieced diamonds and a solid diamond. This quilt was inspired by the logo of the Bluebonnet Quilt Guild of Texas.

Finished Size
Quilt: 83½" x 100½"

Easy-Does-It Feature: Cutting 60° diamonds (see page 24)

Materials
5½ yards black fabric
1¼ yards light green fabric
1¼ yards dark green fabric
1 yard dark fuchsia fabric
¾ yard light fuchsia fabric
½ yard dark purple fabric
½ yard medium purple fabric
¼ yard light purple fabric
1 yard fabric for binding (choose 1 fabric above)
6¼ yards fabric for backing or 3⅛ yards 90"-wide fabric

Cutting
Cut all strips cross-grain. Sufficient yardage is allowed to cut 1 extra strip of each fabric should you find it necessary.
Make templates for patterns X, Y, and Z on pages 98 and 99, following directions on patterns Y and Z to make full-size templates.

From **light purple fabric,** cut:
 2 (2⅛"-wide) strips.
From **medium purple fabric,** cut:
 6 (2⅛"-wide) strips.
From **dark purple fabric,** cut:
 9 (1¼"-wide) strips.
From **light green fabric,** cut:
 8 (3¼"-wide) strips.
From **dark green fabric,** cut:
 21 (1½"-wide) strips.
  Set aside 8 of these strips for second border.
 8 (1"-wide) strips.

From **light fuchsia fabric,** cut:
 5 (2⅛"-wide) strips.
 10 (1"-wide) strips for third border.
From **dark fuchsia fabric,** cut:
 13 (2⅛"-wide) strips.
From **black fabric,** cut:
 1 (4"-wide) strip.
  From this, cut 10 A triangles as shown in *Diagram 1.*
 8 (3¾"-wide) strips.
  From these, cut 68 B diamonds as shown in *Diagram 2.*
 8 (7"-wide) strips.
  From these, cut 38 C diamonds as shown in *Diagram 3.*
 3 (4¼"-wide) strips.
  From these, cut 14 Ys.
 8 (3"-wide) strips for first border.
 10 (4¼"-wide) strips for fourth border.

The secret to nice set-in seams is to stop and backstitch at each corner dot. Do not stitch through seam allowances. This leaves free-floating seam allowances at intersections that can be pressed flat.

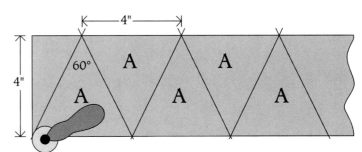

Diagram 1

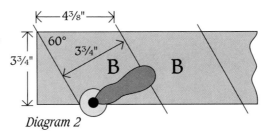

Diagram 2

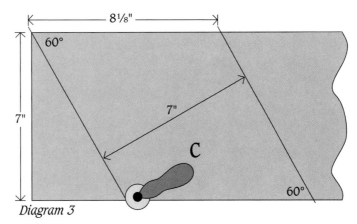

Diagram 3

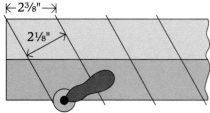

Diagram 4

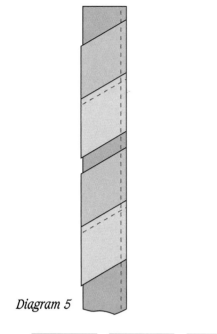

Diagram 5

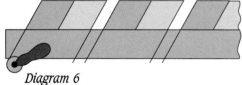

Diagram 6

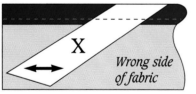

Diagram 7

Piecing Block A

1. With right sides facing, join each light purple strip to a medium purple strip. Press seam allowances toward darker fabric. Referring to *Diagram 4,* cut 36 diamonds for flower center.

2. With right sides facing, align 1 center unit with a medium purple strip, starting 1½" from top of strip as shown in *Diagram 5.* Stitch through both layers. At end of seam, position another unit on strip as shown and continue stitching. Sew all units to medium purple strips in this chain-piecing manner. Press seam allowances toward strips.

3. Referring to *Diagram 6,* align ruler with edge of diamond units and follow angle to rotary-cut strips to get 36 new units. Set aside 2 of these units for partial A blocks.

4. With right sides facing, align left side of 1 unit with a dark purple strip, starting 2¼" from top of strip. Chain-piece 34 units to strips as before. Press seam allowances toward strips; then rotary-cut new units as described in Step 3.

5. Chain-piece opposite side of units to remaining dark purple strips. Press seam allowances toward strips; then trim new units as before. Set flower units aside while making stem unit.

6. Join each light green strip to a 1"-wide strip of dark green to make 8 strip sets. Press seam allowances toward light green strips. Place 2 strip

sets with right sides facing, matching light and dark fabrics. Referring to *Diagram 7,* place Template X on fabric, aligning placement line with strip-set seam. Rotary-cut through both layers to cut 1 X and 1 X reversed. In this manner, cut 34 stem units.

7. Referring to *Block A diagram,* join stem pieces to sides of each flower unit, taking care to stop ¼" from bottom of flower and backstitch. Press seam allowances toward green fabric.

8. Stitch center stem seams, starting at top of stem and backstitching. Press seam allowances open.

9. Chain-piece left side of flower/ stem units to remaining dark green strips, starting 4" from top of strips. Press seam allowances toward strips; then trim units as before. Repeat on right side to complete 34 A blocks.

10. Referring to *Partial A Block diagram,* join 2 remaining center units to A triangles to make 2 partial blocks.

Piecing Block B

1. To make flower units, repeat steps 1–3 above, using strips of light fuchsia and dark fuchsia. Make 71 flower units. Set aside 3 of these for partial blocks.

2. Referring to *Block B diagram,* join flower units to B diamonds. Make 34 B blocks.

3. Referring to *Partial B Block diagram,* join remaining flower units to A triangles to make 3 partial blocks.

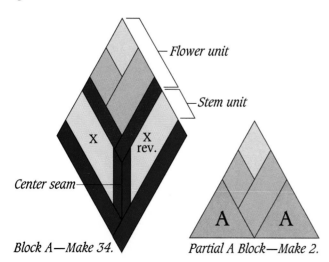

Block A—Make 34.

Partial A Block—Make 2.

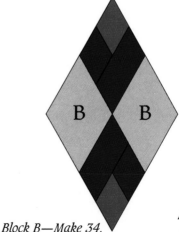

Block B—Make 34.

Partial B Block—Make 3.

Quilt Top Assembly

1. Join 3 A blocks and 3 B blocks to make 1 star as shown in *Star Unit diagram.* Make 10 star units.

2. This quilt is assembled in a continuous manner, similar to patterns such as Double Wedding Ring or Grandmother's Fan. Referring to *Quilt Top Assembly Diagram,* join star units with set-in C diamonds. (Bold lines indicate suggested piecing units.) Use remaining blocks, partial blocks, and Y triangles to fill in at edges as shown.

3. For first border, join 3"-wide black strips to make 1 (74"-long) strip for top, 2 (83"-long) strips for sides, and 1 (48"-long) strip for bottom.

4. For second border, join 1½"-wide dark green strips to make 1 (78"-long) strip for top, 2 (87"-long) strips for sides, and 1 (52"-long) strip for bottom.

5. For third border, join 1"-wide light fuchsia strips to make 1 (80"-long) strip for top, 2 (89"-long) strips for sides, and 1 (54"-long) strip for bottom.

6. For fourth border, join 4¼"-wide black strips to make 1 (89"-long) strip for top, 2 (99"-long) strips for sides, and 1 (62"-long) strip for bottom.

7. Fold each border strip in half and mark centers. Matching centers, join strips for each border.

8. To join borders to quilt, match center of first border to center of quilt edge. Sew top border on first; then add side borders. Miter top corners. Sew bottom border on last.

9. You should have 1 full strip of each border left over. Join these 4 strips in 1-2-3-4 sequence. From this strip set, cut 1 of Template Z and 1 of Template Z reversed. Referring to *Quilt Top Assembly Diagram,* sew Z pieces to Y triangles at bottom corners; then stitch angled seams to join corners to side and bottom borders.

Star Unit—Make 10.

Partial B Blocks

Quilt Top Assembly Diagram

Partial A Blocks

97

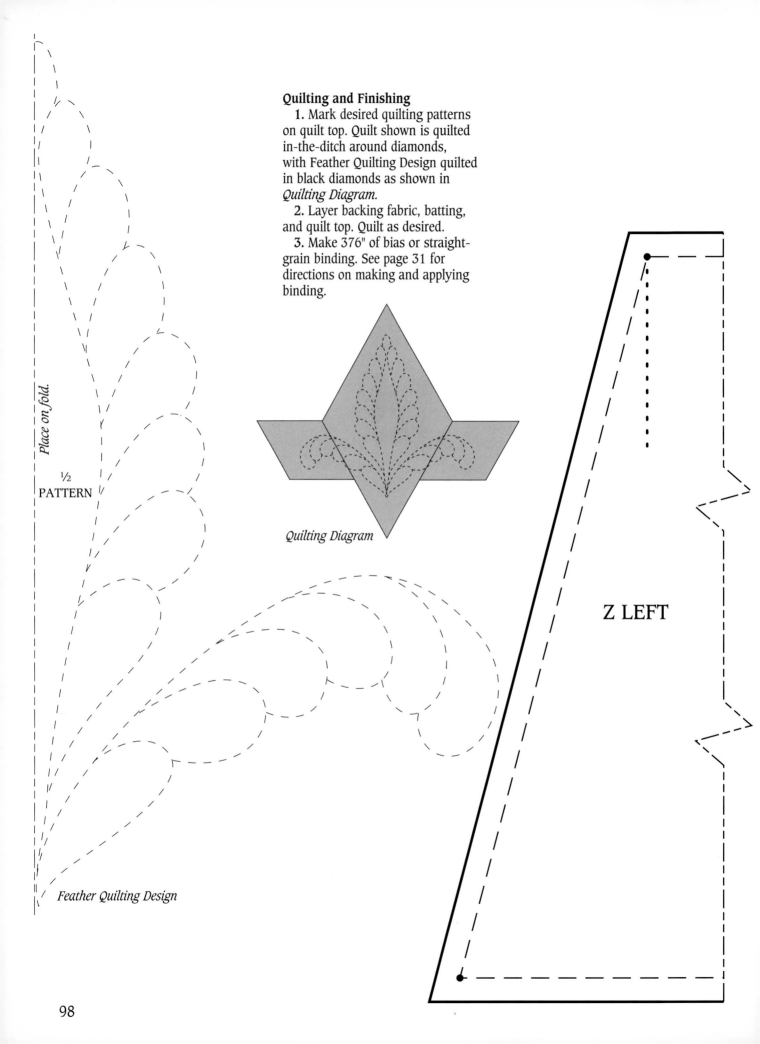

Quilting and Finishing

1. Mark desired quilting patterns on quilt top. Quilt shown is quilted in-the-ditch around diamonds, with Feather Quilting Design quilted in black diamonds as shown in *Quilting Diagram.*

2. Layer backing fabric, batting, and quilt top. Quilt as desired.

3. Make 376" of bias or straight-grain binding. See page 31 for directions on making and applying binding.

Quilting Diagram

Place on fold.

½
PATTERN

Feather Quilting Design

Z LEFT

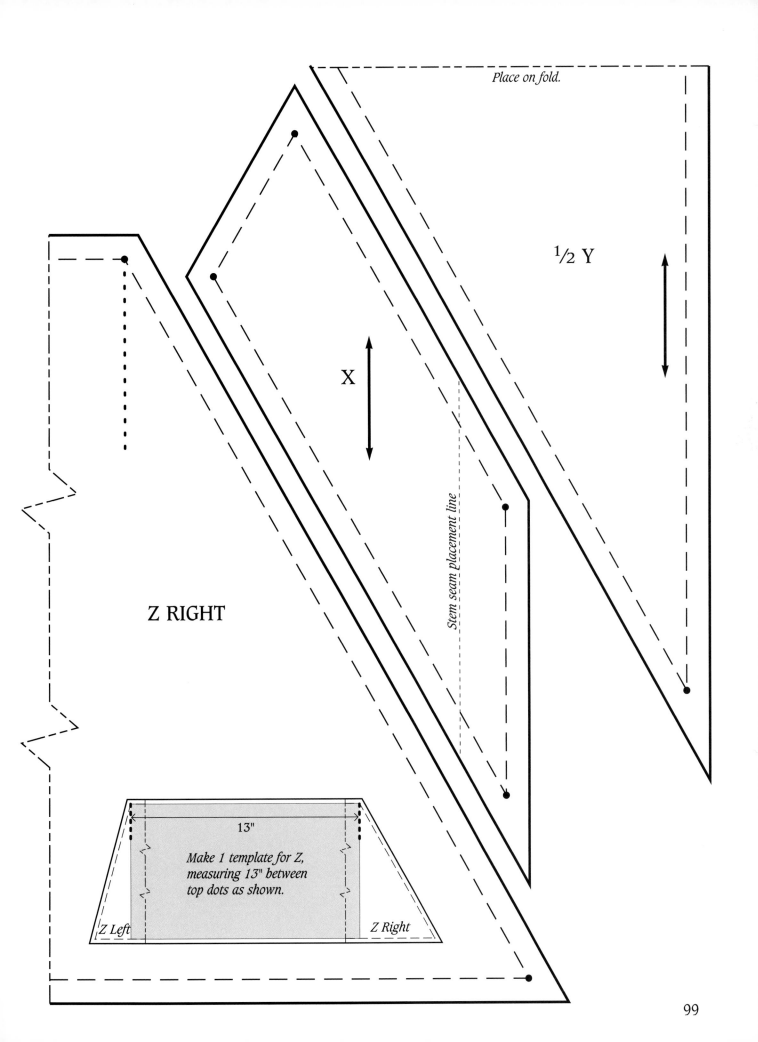

Place on fold.

½ Y

X

Stem seam placement line

Z RIGHT

13"

Make 1 template for Z,
measuring 13" between
top dots as shown.

Z Left

Z Right

a novel
approach

Cuddle Quilts

Spinwheels

McAllister McPuff

Spooling Around

Antique Bow Tie

Bow Tie Doll Quilt

Recycled Tie Wearables

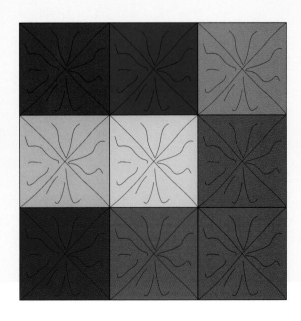

gem from georgia

In making the Cuddle Quilts, I found that 100% polyester polar fleece makes a wonderful substitute for the traditional quilt backing and batting.

Cuddle Quilts

Try your hand at the latest cutting and sewing techniques to create these patchwork samplers. Base all patches on a single color theme to make 3" and 6" blocks and then assemble them as desired into vertical panels. Back your creations with polar fleece for quick and cozy cuddle quilts.

Finished Size
Blocks: Various styles in 3" and 6" widths
Quilt: 58" x 68"

Easy-Does-It Feature: Quick piecing techniques

Materials
1½ yards theme fabric (major print)
½ yard each of 6 coordinated print/solid fabrics
2 yards polar fleece for backing/batting in color to match quilt top
25" square or ⅞ yard fabric for binding (optional)

Quick Four-Patch Blocks
Never, never cut out 1 square at a time when you can cut out a whole strip of squares at once! Determine finished size of squares contained in four-patch blocks and cut strips ½" wider.

For 11 (3") four-patch blocks (made of 1½" squares):
1. From each of 2 contrasting fabrics, cut 1 (2") crosswise strip.
2. Stack strips with right sides facing. Stitch ¼" seam down 1 side. Press seam to darker fabric.
3. Cut band in half crosswise.
4. Stack pieced bands with right sides facing and opposite colors matching *(Diagram 1)*.
5. Draw a line on wrong side of top band every 2" as shown.
6. Stitch ¼" on right-hand side of each mark and at left end of strip. Cut apart on drawn lines. Press blocks.

For 6 (6") four-patch blocks (made of 3" squares):
1. From each of 2 contrasting fabrics, cut 1 (3½") crosswise strip.
2. Follow steps 2–6 above, marking lines every 3½".

Novelty Spinwheels
For 6 (3¾") Spinwheel blocks:
1. Make 6 (6") four-patch blocks as above.
2. Refer to *Spinwheels* quilt on page 107; follow steps 2–4 under Piecing Blocks to twist center of each block.

Half-square Triangles from Strips
To make half-square triangles from strips, cut strips the finished measurement of 1 short side of triangle plus ⅞" (.875).

For 8 (3") half-square triangle blocks:
1. From each of 2 contrasting strips of fabric, cut 1 (3⅞" x 15½") strip.
2. Draw a line on wrong side of 1 strip every 3⅞", creating 4 squares *(Diagram 2)*. Draw 1 diagonal line through each square as shown.
3. Stack strips with right sides facing. Stitch ¼" seam on each side of diagonal line.
4. Cut apart on all drawn lines.
5. Press blocks. Trim dog-ears.

Half-square Triangles from a Square
To make half-square triangles from a square, cut squares ⅞" (.875) larger than the leg of the desired finished triangle.

For 8 (3") half-square triangle blocks:
1. From each of 2 contrasting fabrics, cut 1 (7¾") square.
2. Mark wrong side of 1 square as shown *(Diagram 3)*.
3. With right sides facing and raw edges aligned, lay 1 square on top of the other. Stitch ¼" seam on both sides of each diagonal line.
4. Cut apart on all marked lines.
5. Press blocks. Trim dog-ears.

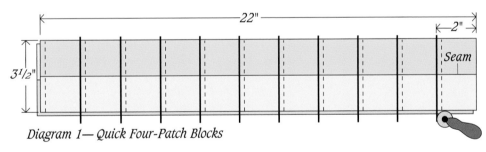

Diagram 1— Quick Four-Patch Blocks

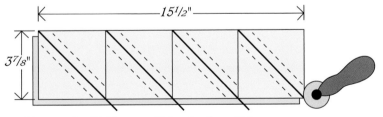

Diagram 2—Half-square Triangles from Strips

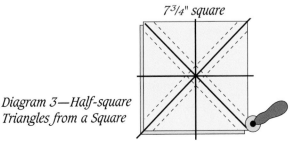

Diagram 3—Half-square Triangles from a Square

Bias-cut Half-square Triangles

To make bias-cut half-square triangles, cut strips the finished width of the square plus ⅞" (.875) x .707. Round the result up to the next ⅛" (see chart on page 105).

For 8 (3") bias-cut half-square triangle blocks:

1. From each of 2 contrasting fabrics, cut 1 (3" x 25") bias strip. (*Hint:* Spray-sizing and pressing help stabilize raw edges. Be sure to press fabric with an up-and-down motion; don't slide iron back and forth over bias edges.)

2. Place strips with right sides facing. Stitch a ¼" seam down each side.

3. Mark 8 right-angle triangles inside bias section using 45° markings on your rotary ruler (*Diagram 4*). See page 24 for more information.

4. Cut apart on all marked lines.

Quarter-square Triangles from Strips

You will make quarter-square triangles using the same basic technique as half-square triangles, except that you will add 1¼" to the finished measurement.

For 20 (3") quarter-square triangle blocks:

1. From each of 2 contrasting fabrics, cut 1 (4¼"-wide) crosswise strip.

2. Draw a line across 1 strip every 4¼".

3. Follow steps 3–5 for making half-square triangles from strips.

4. Stack 2 blocks with right sides facing and opposite colors matching.

5. Draw a diagonal line from corner to corner across seam.

6. Stitch ¼" seam on each side of diagonal line as shown (*Diagram 5*).

7. Cut apart on drawn line.

8. Press blocks (*Diagram 6*). (*Hint:* Press all seams to darker side on first pressing and they will automatically stagger when you join segments to make blocks.)

4-in-1 Flying Geese Rectangles

Pauline Adams of London, England, devised this system for making flying geese. For geese, cut squares the finished height of geese plus 1¼" (.125). For sky, cut squares the finished height of geese plus ⅞" (.875).

For 4 (3"-wide) Flying Geese blocks:

1. From fabric for geese, cut 1 (4¼") square.

2. From sky fabric, cut 4 (2⅜") squares. Mark a diagonal line on wrong side of each square.

3. Refer to steps 4–7 on page 76 to make 4-in-1 Flying Geese.

Migrating Flying Geese

This technique creates a band of mirror-image Flying Geese. For each band, cut twice as many sky squares as geese squares.

For 6"-wide band of 8 Migrating Geese:

1. From goose fabric, cut 4 (5⅜") squares. Cut each in half diagonally to make 8 goose triangles (*Diagram 7*).

2. From sky fabric, cut 4 (5") squares.

3. With right sides facing and corners aligned, place 1 goose triangle in corner of 1 sky square.

4. Sew ¼" seam around 2 outside edges of goose triangle (*Diagram 8*).

5. Draw a diagonal line as shown in *Diagram 9, Figure A*. Cut apart along diagonal line. Open up to reveal 2 mirror images of geese and sky (*Figure B*).

6. Repeat steps 1–5 to make 5 additional units.

7. Lay out units as shown in *Diagram 10*.

8. Join units, sewing from bottom to top, following diagram and aligning geese as you go. Cut 1 extra goose and 1 sky piece to set in as shown in *Diagram 10*. To make top left corner triangle, cut 1 (4¼") square in half diagonally and join to goose.

9. Trim excess sky piece to even bottom (*Diagram 10*).

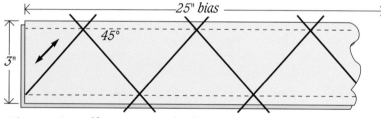

Diagram 4—Half-square Triangles from Bias Strips

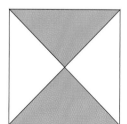

Diagram 5

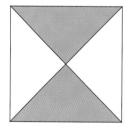

Diagram 6

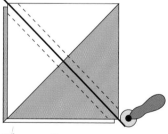

gem from georgia

The quick-piecing methods for each block are a great way to challenge your quilt group to learn a new block process each week, perhaps in a class setting.

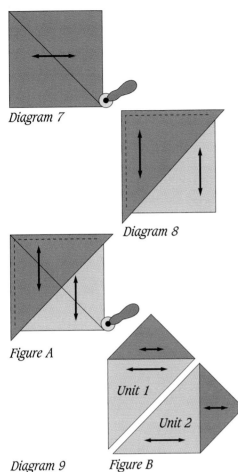

Diagram 7

Diagram 8

Figure A

Diagram 9

Figure B

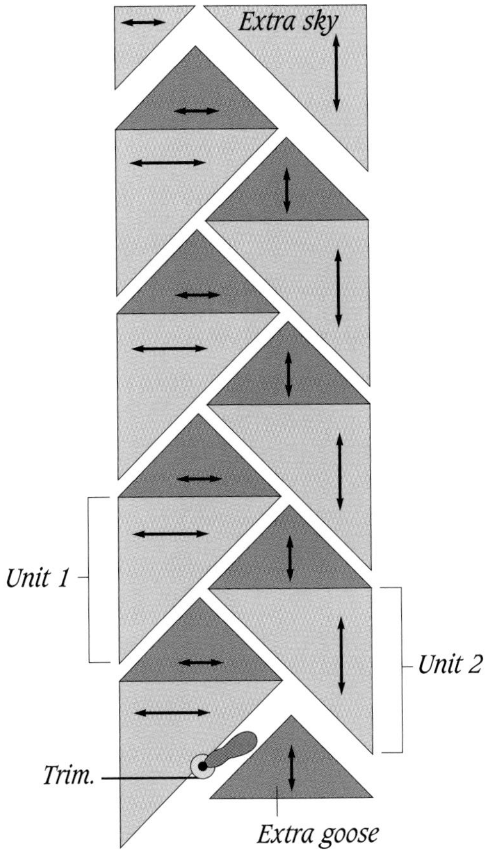

Unit 1

Unit 2

Extra sky

Unit 1

Unit 2

Trim.

Extra goose

Diagram 10

Easy Bow Ties

For each 3" Bow Tie block:

1. From dark fabric, cut 3 (3½") squares.

2. From light fabric, cut 2 (3½") squares.

3. Refer to *Bow Tie Doll Quilt* on page 119; follow steps 2–9 under Piecing Blocks.

Easy Spools

For 2 Spool blocks:

1. From dark fabric, cut 2 (3") squares for centers and 1 (4¼") square. Cut 4¼" square in quarters diagonally.

2. From light fabric, cut 1 (4¼") square. Cut square in quarters diagonally.

3. Refer to *Spooling Around* wall hanging on page 111; follow steps 1–8 under Piecing Blocks.

McAllister McPuff

Try your hand at a couple of square yo-yo's and appliqué them onto coordinated fabrics as accents.

Refer to *McAllister McPuff* on page 109; follow steps 1–3 under Piecing Blocks.

Finishing

1. Pin polar fleece on wall to use as design board. Blocks will adhere to fleece, making it easy to move them around as you adjust your design. Balance color and design as you move blocks into vertical strips. Add any previously made blocks from other quilts that have been waiting to find a home.

2. Cut strips from your 6 coordinating fabrics as spacers between rows and as fillers for any holes in the design. Be sure to add ¼" seam allowance to these strips.

3. Stitch pieces into 68"-long vertical rows. Make enough vertical rows to span the width of your polar fleece (usually 58" to 60" wide).

4. Stitch vertical rows together. Stack pieced top, right side up, on polar fleece. No batting is needed. Machine quilting is a must with this heavy fleece backing. Quilt in-the-ditch or

an all-over design. Finish edges with bias binding, or by turning edges of fleece and patchwork under and top-stitching around edges.

Bias Half Squares

Desired Size of Finished Square	Width of Bias to Cut
1"	1⅜"
1¼"	1½"
1½"	1⅝"
1¾"	1⅞"
2"	2"
2¼"	2¼"
2½"	2⅜"
2¾"	2⅝"
3"	2¾"
3¼"	3"
3½"	3⅛"
3¾"	3¼"
4"	3½"
4¼"	3⅝"
4½"	3⅞"
4¾"	4"
5"	4⅛"
5¼"	4⅜"
5½"	4½"
5¾"	4¾"
6"	4⅞"
6¼"	5"
6½"	5¼"
6¾"	5⅜"
7"	5⅝"
7¼"	5¾"
7½"	6"
7¾"	6⅛"
8"	6¼"
8¼"	6½"
8½"	6⅝"
8¾"	6¾"
9"	7"
9¼"	7⅛"
9½"	7⅜"
9¾"	7½"
10"	7¾"
10¼"	7⅞"
10½"	8"
10¾"	8¼"
11"	8⅜"
11¼"	8⅝"
11½"	8¾"
11¾"	8⅞"
12"	9⅛"

Spinwheels

gem from georgia

Sewing consecutive patchwork, as in chain piecing, without cutting threads is a great time-saver.

Spinwheels

A tuck at the edge, a twist in the middle, and a simple four-patch takes on a whole new character. The texture and dimension in this block make it ideal alone or in small groups for quilted clothing.

Finished Size
Blocks: 20 (2¼") blocks
Quilt: 16½" x 19½"

Easy-Does-It Feature: Chain piecing

Materials
⅓ yard total of assorted pastel prints (each at least 2" x 4")
⅜ yard muslin
⅔ yard pastel print for binding and backing

Cutting
From **assorted pastel prints**, cut:
   20 pairs of 2" squares (40 total).
   Note: Each pair should be from same fabric.
   44 (2") squares for border.
   17" x 20" rectangle for backing.
From **muslin**, cut:
   12 (2¾") inside setting squares.
   18 (3¼") outside setting squares.
   40 (2") squares.

Piecing Blocks
   1. With right sides facing, chain-piece each 2" pastel square with a 2" muslin square. Press seams toward pastel squares. Then chain-piece units so that matching colors are in opposite corners to make 20 four-patch squares. Press, staggering seams.
   2. At every seam, make a ⅜" tuck. Fold each tuck in same direction *(Diagram 1)*.
   3. Twist center fabric to create center square set on point within larger square *(Diagram 2)*. Press.

   4. To secure tucks, stitch across seam allowance at outside edges and tack at center. Repeat for each square. *(Hint:* Drop feed dogs and use small zigzag stitch to tack center of each block by machine.)

Quilt Top Assembly
   1. Arrange blocks on point and alternate with 2¾" muslin setting squares, rotating pieced blocks within each row as shown *(Diagram 3)*.
   2. Stitch blocks into 8 diagonal rows, with 3¼" muslin squares sewn into the perimeter and the corners as shown.
   3. Join rows.
   4. Trim quilt top to 14" x 17" *(Diagram 4)*.
   5. Join 9 squares each for top and bottom borders and 13 squares each for side borders *(Diagram 5)*. Join borders to quilt.

Quilting and Finishing
   Note: Doll-sized quilts look best with very thin batting. Splitting a batt often works well.
   1. Layer quilt top, batting, and backing. Baste.
   2. Quilt in-the-ditch between border and blocks.
   3. Quilt a simple spiral in center of each setting block.
   4. Cut pastel print into 2 (1½"-wide) crosswise strips. Join strips to make straight-grain binding. See page 31 for instructions on making and applying binding.

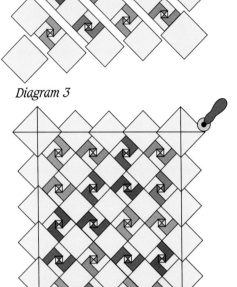

Diagram 3

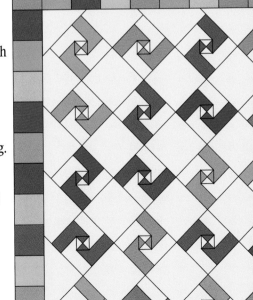

Diagram 4

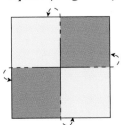

Diagram 1

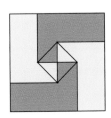

Diagram 2

Diagram 5

McAllister McPuff

McAllister McPuff

From Scotland's Isle of Arran comes this novelty block. With great joy, I machine-stitched and my mother joined the 224 blocks in this quilt for my first grandchild and her first great-grandchild.

Finished Size
Blocks: 224 (4") yo-yo blocks
Quilt: 56" x 64"

Easy-Does-It Feature: Square yo-yo

Materials
11" squares of scrap fabric: 112 light
 and 112 dark
Full-size batting
Heavy-duty thread

Cutting
Make template on page 110.
From **light scraps,** cut:
 112 pieces, using template.
From **dark scraps,** cut:
 112 pieces, using template.
From **batting,** cut:
 224 (4") squares.

Piecing Blocks
1. With right sides facing, fold 1 shape to align 2 adjacent edges *(Block Diagram).* Join edges from bottom dot up to top dot. Backstitch. Repeat to stitch each edge of each shape.

2. Center 4" square of batting on wrong side of each puff. Pin from right side (inside) of puff. Turn right side out. Remove pins.

3. Turn raw edges at top under ¼". Using heavy-duty thread, take ¼"-long gathering stitches along top edge of each shape. Pull thread to gather. Secure each square by stitching through to back of square when knotting thread off. Press to form squares.

Quilt Top Assembly
1. Arrange squares into 16 horizontal rows of 14 blocks each. Arrange dark and light blocks according to *Quilt Top Assembly Diagram.*

2. Pin squares together, tugging at corners to be sure all fullness falls to center.

3. Join blocks in each row with narrow zigzag (about ⅛" wide).

4. Join rows with same zigzag stitch. *Note:* There is no binding, backing, or quilting on this novelty quilt.

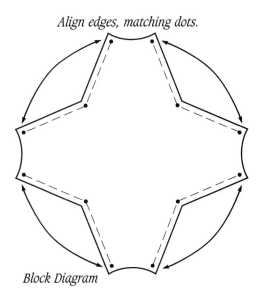

Align edges, matching dots.

Block Diagram

Quilt Top Assembly Diagram

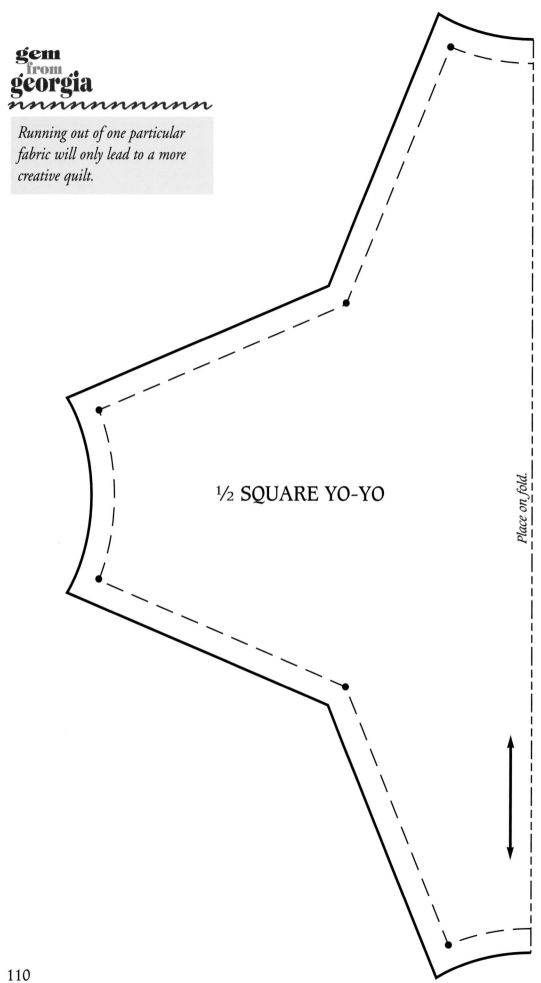

Running out of one particular fabric will only lead to a more creative quilt.

½ SQUARE YO-YO

Place on fold.

Spooling Around

Spooling around in my sewing room led to this new twist on the spools block. Folded and sewn into place, these spools form tiny pockets to hold small sewing notions.

Spooling Around

Finished Size
Blocks: 6 (8") and 11 (4") blocks
Wall Hanging: 20" x 29¾"

Easy-Does-It Feature: Easy spool blocks

Materials
⅞ yard black fabric
⅞ yard white fabric
¾ yard total of various print fabric scraps
Batting
⅝ yard fabric for backing
Yardstick cut to 22" and drilled with small hole ½" from each end
½ yard each of ⅛"-wide ribbon in 4 colors to match fabrics
Spools and other sewing notions for trim

Cutting
Hint: Stack fabrics for several spools and cut at same time.
From **black fabric**, cut:
  2 (9¼") squares. Cut each into quarters diagonally for large spools (you will have 2 triangles left over).
  3 (5¼") squares. Cut each into quarters diagonally for small spools (you will have 2 triangles left over).
  1 (4" x 21") rectangle for hanging sleeve.
From **white fabric**, cut:
  2 (9¼") squares. Cut each into quarters diagonally for large spools (you will have 2 triangles left over).
  3 (5¼") square. Cut each into quarters diagonally for small spools.
From **each print fabric**, cut:
  1 (8") square each for centers of 6 large spools.
  3 (9¼") squares for ends of all 6 large spools. Cut each into quarters diagonally.
  1 (4") square each for centers of 11 small spools.
  6 (5¼") squares for ends of all 11 small spools. Cut each into quarters diagonally (you will have 2 left over).
From **each satin ribbon**, cut:
  1 (43") and 2 (10") lengths.

111

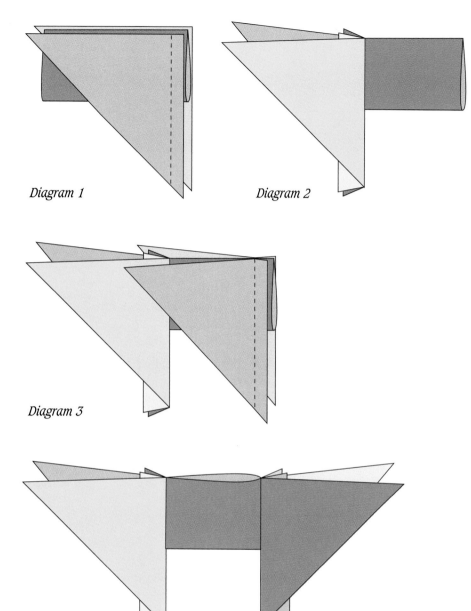

Diagram 1

Diagram 2

Diagram 3

Diagram 4

Piecing Blocks

1. For 1 large Spool block: Fold 1 (8") print square in half with wrong sides facing to make a rectangle.

2. With right sides facing and raw edges aligned, sandwich rectangle between 1 large white and 1 large matching print triangle *(Diagram 1)*.

3. Stitch across 1 edge as shown, catching short end of rectangle in seam.

4. Unfold and press both triangles away from rectangle *(Diagram 2)*.

5. Sandwich other end of rectangle between next large white and matching print triangles. *Note:* Color order should be opposite of first pair.

6. Stitch across edge, catching short end of rectangle in seam. *(Diagram 3)*. Unfold and press both triangles away from rectangle to form a "bridge" *(Diagram 4)*.

7. Open rectangle and refold pieces as shown, aligning all raw edges and seam lines *(Diagram 5)*. Stitch across top edge, staggering seams.

8. Open block and press. Center of spool forms naturally *(Diagram 6)*. Twirl seams in intersection (see page 23). Trim dog-ears.

9. Referring to photograph and *Assembly Diagram,* repeat to make 6 large spools (3 with black triangles and 3 with white) and 11 small spools (5 with black triangles and 6 with white).

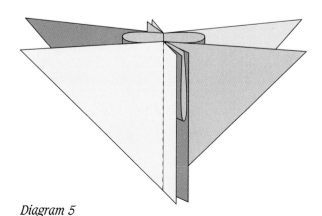

Diagram 5

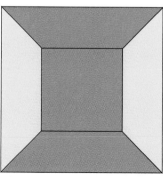

Diagram 6

Assembly

1. Arrange large and small spool blocks according to *Assembly Diagram.*

2. Join small spools within each section first and then join to large spools. Make 3 sections as indicated.

3. Join sections.

Quilting and Finishing

1. To make hanging sleeve: Fold under ½" on each short end of 4" x 21" rectangle and press. Baste or pin in place.

2. With wrong sides facing and raw edges aligned, fold sleeve in half lengthwise. With raw edges aligned, place sleeve at top of wall hanging front. Stitch.

3. Fold each 10" length of ribbon in half. Position ribbons along bottom of wall hanging, with folded edges aligned with raw edges of wall hanging. Pin in place.

4. Pin batting to wrong side of backing fabric.

5. Stack backing and wall hanging with right sides facing. Stitch around all 4 sides, leaving an 8" opening along 1 side. Turn. Slipstitch opening closed.

6. Machine-quilt in-the-ditch between blocks and ⅛" from outer edges.

7. Slip yardstick through hanging sleeve.

8. To make ribbon hanger: Holding all 4 ribbons together as 1, thread ends of 43" strands of ribbon through hole in 1 end of yardstick. Knot ends to secure. Thread spools onto free end of ribbons, knotting between spools. Thread ribbon ends through remaining hole in yardstick. Knot ends.

9. Tie spools to ribbons at bottom of wall hanging (see photo).

10. Add sewing notions to finished hanging.

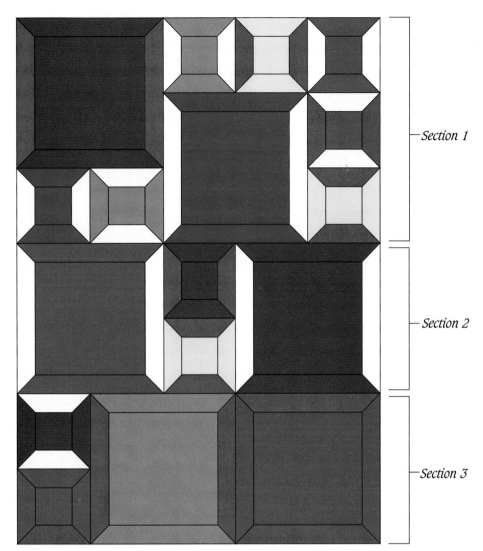

Section 1

Section 2

Section 3

Assembly Diagram

Always display a quilted project away from direct sunlight to prevent fading. A quilt should hang for no more than three months, and then it needs to rest a while.

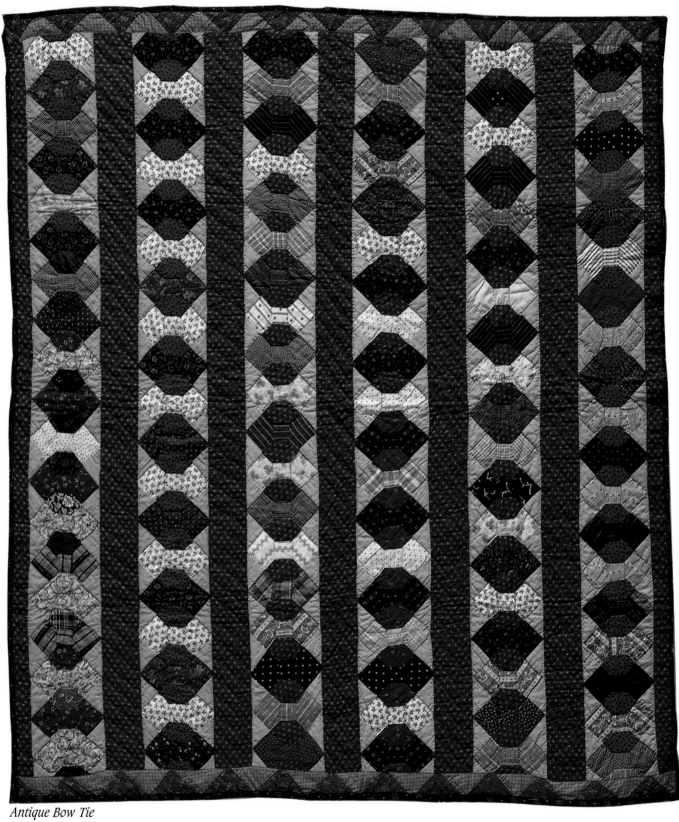

Antique Bow Tie

114

Antique Bow Tie

If this quilt could talk, what stories it would tell! Irene Houg inherited the quilt from her grandmother, Ingeborg Ness. Irene recalls a time when she visited her grandmother's farm during an electrical storm. Her grandmother, who had been frightened of storms ever since her home and barn were destroyed by fire, always hid in the bed during bad weather. What comfort this quilt provided then!

Finished Size
Quilt: 75½" x 86¾"

Easy-Does-It Feature: Set-in seams

Materials
1 yard assorted prints for hexagons (A, F)
Scraps totaling 2¼ yards for bow ties (B, C)
1⅛ yards bright yellow for side triangles (D, E)
2 yards print for sashing strips
½ yard red print for border triangles (G)
½ yard bubblegum pink for border triangles (G)
5 yards fabric for backing
29" square fabric for binding

Cutting
Make templates for patterns A, B, C, and F on page 117.
From **prints for hexagons,** cut:
   108 As and 12 Fs.
From **scraps for bow ties,** cut:
   114 Bs and 228 Cs (each B should have 2 matching Cs).
From **bright yellow,** cut:
   7 (5½"-wide) strips. Cut strips into 57 (5½") squares. Cut squares into quarters diagonally to make 228 quarter-square triangles. Set 216 of these aside for side triangles (D). Cut 12 remaining triangles in half again to make 24 triangles (E) for row ends.

From **print for sashing strips,** cut:
   6 (4½" x 80½") strips for sashing strips. Cut 1 strip in half lengthwise for side borders.
From **red print,** cut:
   7 (7¼") squares. Cut squares into quarters diagonally to make 28 quarter-square triangles (G). (You will have 2 left over.)
From **bubblegum pink,** cut:
   7 (7¼") squares. Cut each square into quarters diagonally to make 28 quarter-square triangles (G). (You will have 2 left over.)

Piecing Blocks
Hint: The secret to accurate set-in seams is to stitch to the corner dot, stop, backstitch a couple of stitches, and then break off the thread. Begin stitching at the corner dot on the other side of the seam allowance. This technique permits a free-floating seam.

   1. Join long side of 2 Es to long side of 2 Cs *(Diagram 1)*.
   2. Join inside of each C to 1 B *(Diagram 2)*.
   3. Join F to top of unit and A to bottom of unit, using set-in seams, to complete 1 bow tie *(Diagram 3)*.
   4. To add next bow tie, join 1 B to short side of A in pieced unit. Join 2 Ds to 2 Cs; join these to pieced unit *(Diagram 4)*. Continue in this manner until 19 bow ties are connected *(Diagram 5)*. End row with 1 F and 2 Es as shown. Repeat to make 6 rows.

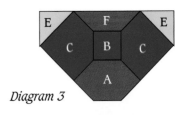

Diagram 3

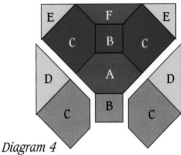

Diagram 4

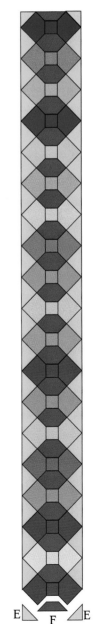

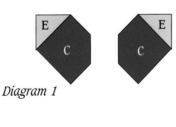

Diagram 1

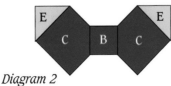

Diagram 2

Diagram 5

Quilt Top Assembly

1. Referring to *Quilt Top Assembly Diagram,* join 4½"-wide sashing strips between the 6 pieced rows. Add 2¼"-wide strips to outer edges for side borders.

2. Alternating colors, join 26 Gs as shown in *Diagram 6* for bottom border. Repeat to make top border. Matching centers, join borders to quilt, trimming excess at sides.

Quilting and Finishing

1. Layer quilt top, batting, and backing. Baste. Outline-quilt around bow ties and quilt diagonal lines in borders.

2. Make 320" of bias binding from 29" square. See page 31 for directions on making and applying binding.

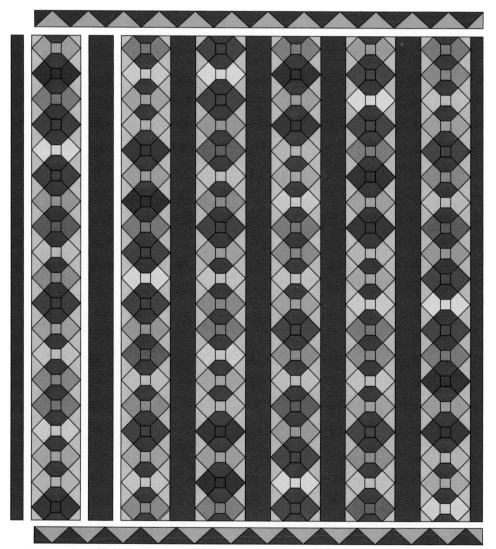

Diagram 6

gem from georgia
𝓷𝓷𝓷𝓷𝓷𝓷𝓷𝓷

Quilters of the past did not have the luxury of rotary cutters and acrylic rulers that we enjoy today. You may notice in the photo of Antique Bow Tie *that several triangle points are cut off and the sashing strips are slightly uneven. If you follow the directions given here, you should have sharp points and straight lines. Also, the border triangles (G) are all a uniform size, so your top and bottom border strips will be longer than needed. Simply trim your borders to fit your quilt.*

Quilt Top Assembly Diagram

116

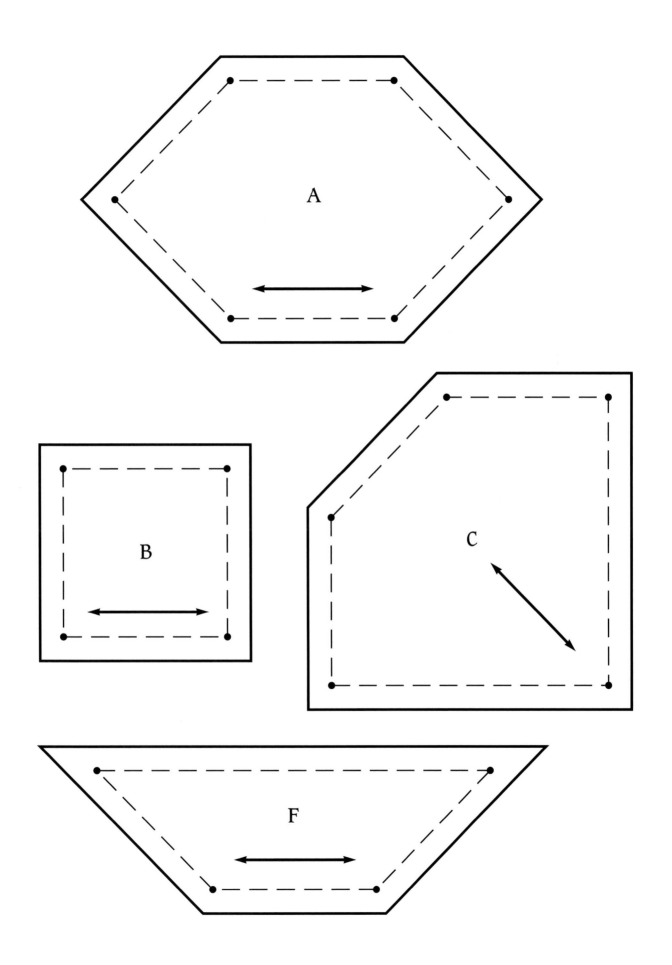

Bow Tie Doll Quilt

Bow Tie Doll Quilt

This charming doll quilt features tiny calico Bow Ties made with my Easy-Does-It method. What a great way to show off that antique doll bed.

Finished Size
Blocks: 18 (3") blocks
Quilt: 18¼" x 22½"

Easy-Does-It Feature: Easy Bow Ties

Materials
18 (6"-square or larger) assorted pastel prints
1½ yards muslin for blocks, backing, and binding
Thin batting

Cutting
From **pastel prints,** cut:
3 (2") squares from each print (18 groups of 3, or 54 squares total).
1¼"-wide strips of various lengths to total about 67½" for inner borders.
From **muslin,** cut:
36 (2") squares for background.
3 (5½") squares. Cut in quarters diagonally to make 12 side triangles (you will have 2 left over).
2 (3") squares. Cut in half diagonally to make 4 corner triangles.
2 (2½" x 19½") strips for outer side borders.
2 (2½" x 19") strips for outer top and bottom borders.
1 (20" x 24¾") rectangle for backing.
2 (1½" x 23¾") strips for side binding.
2 (1½" x 19½") strips for top and bottom binding.

Piecing Blocks
1. Select 3 (2") print squares of same fabric and 2 (2") muslin squares.
2. With wrong sides facing, fold 1 print square in half to make a 1" x 2" rectangle.
3. Sandwich rectangle between 1 print and 1 muslin square, with right sides facing and raw edges aligned *(Diagram 1)*.
4. Stitch across 1 edge as shown, catching short end of rectangle in seam.
5. Unfold and press both squares away from rectangle *(Diagram 2)*.
6. Sandwich other end of rectangle between next print and muslin squares. *Note:* Print and muslin order should be opposite of first pair.

Diagram 1

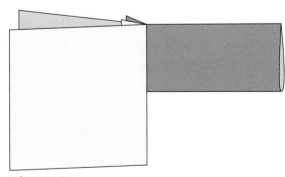

Diagram 2

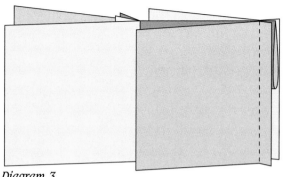

Diagram 3

7. Stitch across edge, catching short end of rectangle in seam *(Diagram 3)*. Unfold and press both squares away from rectangle to form a "bridge" *(Diagram 4)*.

8. Open rectangle and refold pieces as shown, aligning all raw edges and seam lines *(Diagram 5)*. Stitch top edge, staggering seams *(Diagram 6)*.

9. Press block. Bow tie knot forms naturally *(Diagram 7)*. Twirl seams in intersection (see page 23).

10. Repeat to make 18 Bow Tie blocks.

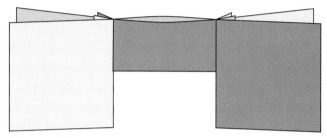

Diagram 4

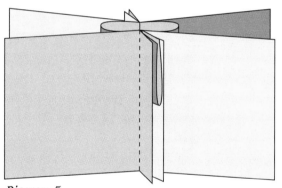

Diagram 5

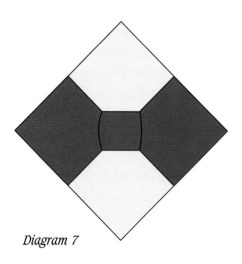

Diagram 7

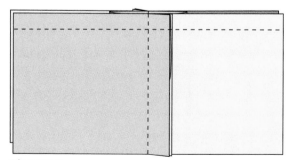

Diagram 6

Quilt Top Assembly

1. Arrange blocks on point as shown *(Diagram 8)*.

2. Place side triangles at end of each row and corner triangles in each corner.

3. Join blocks in diagonal rows.

4. Join rows.

5. For inner borders, join various lengths of 1¼"-wide print strips to make 2 (18½"-long) strips and 2 (20"-long) strips.

6. Join 20" strips to sides of quilt. Then join 18½" strips to top and bottom *(Quilt Diagram)*.

7. For outer borders, join 2½" x 19½" muslin strips to each side of quilt. Join 2½" x 19" muslin strips to top and bottom of quilt, trimming excess as needed.

Quilting and Finishing

Note: Doll-sized quilts look best with very thin batting. Splitting a batt often works well.

1. Layer quilt top, batting, and backing. Baste.

2. Outline-quilt all blocks. Quilt a heart in each end of bow tie. Quilt borders as desired.

3. Bind with straight-grain binding (see page 32).

Diagram 8

Quilt Diagram

Woven Jacket Front

Woven Jacket Back

122

Recycled Tie Wearables

The news is out about the easiest way to reuse Daddy's ties. Since ties are made on the bias, they need no hemming when cut apart. Use strips to weave a colorful jacket accent. And because vests are a must for today's wardrobe, I've included two eyecatching designs—one woven and one appliquéd.

Easy-Does-It Feature: Machine appliqué

Woven Jacket
Materials
Jacket pattern of your choice
Denim, wool, melton, corduroy, or Ultrasuede in amount called for in pattern
Lightweight lining fabric in amount called for in pattern
2 yards fusible tricot interfacing
Approximately 20 cleaned neckties
Approximately 90" rib knit tubing for neck, arms, and waistband (amount varies with size and style of jacket—see pattern)
Heavy-duty separating jacket-style zipper (length according to jacket pattern)

Cutting
1. Cut out all jacket and lining pieces. Set lining aside.
2. Cut ties lengthwise into 1½"-wide strips. (Width can vary as desired.)

Constructing Jacket
1. Lay all jacket pieces out flat. Slash openings with rotary cutter in selected areas of sleeves, back, and fronts *(Diagrams 1–3)*. Slashes will be framework for weaving. Do not slash to edge of jacket pieces. Leave 2" to 3" of fabric uncut around outside edge of each piece to provide a stable edge for joining to other pieces.

Note: Space slashes as desired. Arrangement can be diagonal or straight, symmetrical or asymmetrical. Those pictured are 1½" apart. Consider tendency of your jacket fabric to ravel when choosing to cut with crosswise grain or straight-of-the-grain. For fabric that tends to ravel, make diagonal cuts. For fabric that does not ravel easily, either diagonal or straight-grain cuts work well.

2. Weave strips in and out of slashes in jacket pieces as desired *(Diagram 4)*. Secure ends of each strip with pins.

3. Remove pins. Press fusible tricot interfacing on wrong side of each woven area to stabilize piece.

4. Embellish selected areas with decorative machine stitches as shown in photo. *Note:* I used metallic thread for the decorative stitching on this jacket.

5. Construct jacket and lining according to pattern instructions.

6. With right sides facing, join jacket and lining along front seams *(Diagram 5)*. Turn.

7. With wrong sides facing, align and pin raw edges of lining to raw edges of jacket.

8. Using a serger or machine-zigzag, attach rib knit tubing to raw edges of neck, arms, and waist.

9. Attach zipper to front opening according to zipper directions.

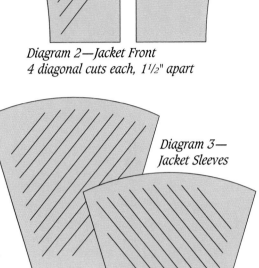

Diagram 2—Jacket Front
4 diagonal cuts each, 1½" apart

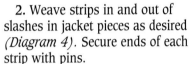

Diagram 3—Jacket Sleeves

11 diagonal cuts each, 1½" apart

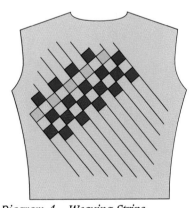

Diagram 4—Weaving Strips

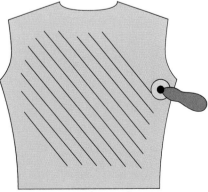

Diagram 1—Jacket Back
11 diagonal cuts, 1½" apart

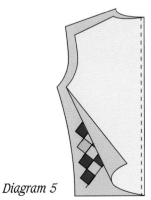

Diagram 5

Woven Vest

Woven Vest

Make a woven vest in same manner as jacket, except secure ends of tie strips on outside with decorative buttons. Bind edges with bias made from ties (see photo at left).

Appliquéd Vest
Materials

Scraps from cleaned neckties
Lined-vest pattern of your choice
Fabric in amount called for in pattern
Coordinated fabric for lining
Metallic thread in assorted colors
½ yard paper-backed fusible web
Cotton flannel (prewashed) or lightweight batting for interlining

Cutting

1. Cut out vest, lining, and interlining pieces according to pattern. Set lining and interlining aside.

2. To cut appliqué shapes, use templates A, B, and C to trace about 15 assorted shapes on paper side of fusible web. (If larger appliqués are desired, add ¼" to ½" around outside edge of templates.) Cut out shapes slightly larger than drawn.

3. Press shapes to wrong side of tie scraps. Cut out each shape along traced line. Peel off paper backing.

Constructing Vest

1. Arrange appliqués on vest panels. (*Hint:* Pin your vest on a wall or on a hanger to imagine how it will look when worn.) Press in place.

2. With metallic threads, cover all raw edges of shapes with decorative machine or hand embroidery stitches (see photos below).

3. Join shoulder seams.

4. Pin interlining to wrong side of lining and treat as 1 fabric. Join shoulder seams in lining/interlining.

5. To make "button" loops, cut 1 (1" x 5") bias strip from each of 2 tie scraps. With right sides facing, fold strips in half lengthwise, stitch along long edge, and turn. Fold each strip in half to form a loop. With raw edges aligned, stitch loops to right side of right jacket front (see photo).

6. Construct vest, following pattern instructions.

7. Overcast finished edges with metallic thread.

8. Using metallic thread, echo-quilt around several shapes to secure all layers.

9. To make 1 bow tie "button," cut 1 (4") square from tie scrap. With right sides facing, fold square in half and stitch long edge and 1 end. Turn. Fold raw end under ¼" and slipstitch closed. Pinch fabric in center to make a bow tie and tack in place. Repeat to make a second button. Stitch buttons to left side of vest opposite loops (see photo).

Appliquéd Vest

A

B

C

Take a Seat

Replace worn-out chair seats with discarded ties for a quick, colorful decorating update. First, secure ties to the chair side-by-side horizontally, creating the warp. Secure the next set of ties side-by-side vertically to the chair, weaving them over and under the warp set. Tie all in tight, secure knots under the seat. Weave tie ends under the seat bottom, or let them dangle underneath.

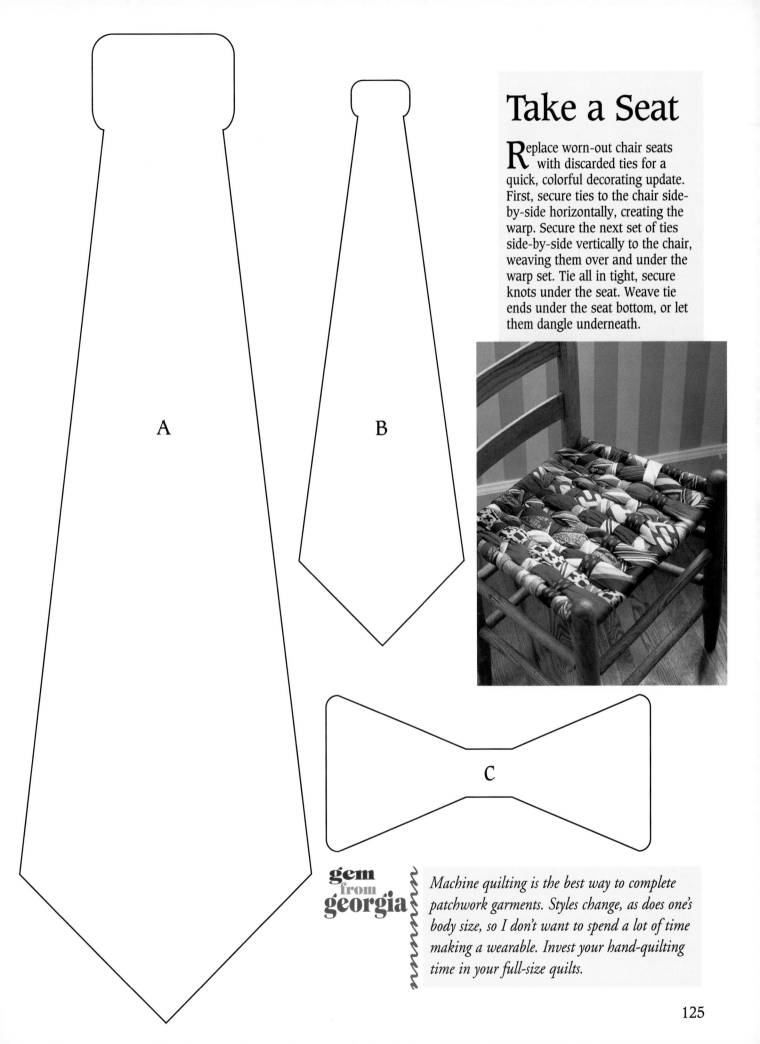

gem from georgia

Machine quilting is the best way to complete patchwork garments. Styles change, as does one's body size, so I don't want to spend a lot of time making a wearable. Invest your hand-quilting time in your full-size quilts.

warming up the world

Ukrainian Dolls

Ukrainian Dolls Wall Hanging

Yackety Yack

Tartan Thistle

Thistle Table Topper

Tartan Thistle Vest

Quilting Around the World

Tuxedo Friendship

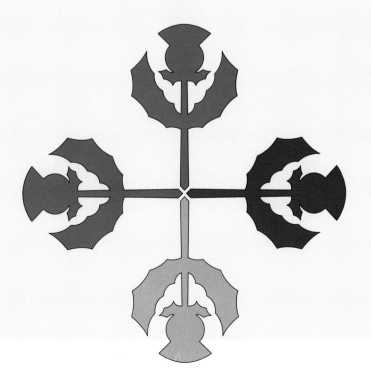

Ukrainian Dolls

Ukrainian Dolls

I created this quilt in 1994 at the request of Middfest International Foundation of Middleton, Ohio. An organization dedicated to sharing international cultures, Middfest honored the eastern European country of Ukraine at its annual festival.

Finished Size
Quilt: 90" x 100"

Easy-Does-It Feature: Continuous bias

Materials
4 yards tan fabric for shelf background and inner border
4 yards striped fabric for outer border
2 yards orange fabric for middle border and shelf tops
1 yard dark brown fabric for shelf sides
1 yard medium brown fabric for shelf base
¾ yard muslin for doll faces
16 (8" x 13") assorted scraps for large dolls
16 (7" x 11") assorted scraps for medium dolls
16 (5" x 9") assorted scraps for small dolls
Scraps or ¼ yard black fabric for hair
⅞ yard fabric for binding
3 yards 108"-wide fabric for backing
Black embroidery floss for facial features
Water-soluble marker
Pink fine-tip permanent marker

Cutting
Cut all strips cross-grain except as noted.
From **tan fabric**, cut:
  8 (15½" x 30½") pieces for shelf background.
  2 (2½" x 80½") lengthwise strips and 2 (2½" x 68½") lengthwise strips for inner borders.
From **medium brown fabric**, cut:
  8 (4½" x 34½") strips for shelf base.

From **dark brown fabric**, cut:
  4 (4½"-wide) strips. From these, cut 8 (4½" x 19½") pieces for shelf sides.
  1 (18") square for bias trim for shelf tops.
From **orange fabric**, cut:
  8 (3½" x 34½") strips for shelf tops.
  8 (3½"-wide) strips for middle border.
  2 (5½" x 7½") pieces for bottom border (cabinet legs).
From **black fabric**, cut:
  6 (1¼"-wide) strips for hair.
From **striped fabric**, cut:
  2 (7½" x 40") strips for top border.
  2 (7½" x 35") strips for bottom border.
  2 (6½" x 100½") lengthwise strips for side borders.

Making Shelf
1. Join 2 (15½" x 30¼") tan pieces at 1 end to make 1 (15½" x 60½") panel.

2. Matching top edges, sew a dark brown side piece to each side of tan panel. Stop sewing ¼" from end of seam, letting dark brown fabric extend beyond bottom of tan panel.

3. Join 2 strips of medium brown fabric end-to-end to make a 4½" x 68½" strip. With right sides facing and matching center seams, pin this strip to bottom of tan shelf panel. Stitch strip to shelf panel as shown in *Shelf Diagram,* starting and ending seam ¼" from corners of tan panel. Miter bottom corners.

4. Repeat steps 1–4 to make 3 more shelves.

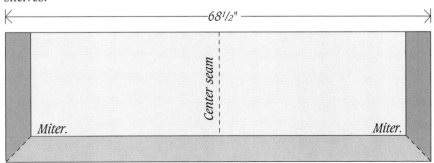

Shelf Diagram

Making Shelf Top

Make template of Shelf Top Arch pattern on page 131.

1. Referring to instructions on page 31, make 280" of 1"-wide continuous bias from 18" square of dark brown fabric. With wrong sides facing, fold bias in half lengthwise and press. Cut 4 (70"-long) strips, 1 for each shelf.

2. Join 2 (3½" x 34½") orange strips to make 1 (3½" x 68½") strip for shelf top.

3. With wrong sides facing, fold strip in half at center seam, matching ends as shown in *Diagram 1*. Measure 2¼" from ends and mark with pins. Fold strip in half again, bringing center seam to marked line, as shown in *Diagram 2*. Fold once more, bringing right-hand fold to marked line as shown in *Diagram 3*. You will have 8 layers of fabric, except at ends, where you will have 2 layers.

4. Lay Shelf Top Arch template on folded strip, aligning straight edge at top and bottom of template with fabric and ends of template with folds of fabric *(Diagram 4)*. Cut bottom curved edge of strip through all layers to make arches.

5. With right sides facing and raw edges aligned, pin 1 (70") bias strip to bottom (curved) edge of shelf top. Stitch through all layers, ¼" from raw edge. Turn seam allowance up and press in place so ¼" of bias trim shows beyond finished edge of arches.

6. Matching top edges and center seams, pin shelf top to shelf panel, with both pieces right side up. Top-stitch in-the-ditch along bias trim seam line to join shelf top to shelf panel. Trim tan fabric behind shelf top, leaving ¼" seam allowance.

7. Repeat steps 2–6 to make 3 more shelves.

Preparing Doll Faces

1. Using a water-soluble marker, lightly trace 16 of *each* face onto muslin, using face patterns on pages 132 and 133. Trace hair lines on each face. Do not cut out faces yet.

2. Using 2 strands of floss, embroider faces with outline stitch. Color in cheeks with pink permanent pen.

3. Adding ¼" seam allowances, cut out faces.

4. With right sides facing, position a hair strip over traced line on each head as shown in *Hair Placement Diagram*. Stitch. Flip strip to right side and press. Trim excess strip. Repeat with second strip on each head. Trim hair strips to match curve of head. Remove any visible markings.

Appliquéing Dolls

Make template for each doll pattern on pages 132 and 133.

1. Adding ¼" seam allowance, cut 16 of each doll shape from assorted print fabrics.

2. Adding seam allowance, cut out face opening in each doll. Turn seam allowance under and baste.

3. Position a muslin face under each opening, aligning seam lines. Appliqué faces in place.

4. Referring to photograph, arrange dolls in groups of 3. Pin dolls on shelves and appliqué in place. (*Note:* If desired, machine-stitch each group of dolls together along adjoining edges and then appliqué as 1 piece onto foundation.)

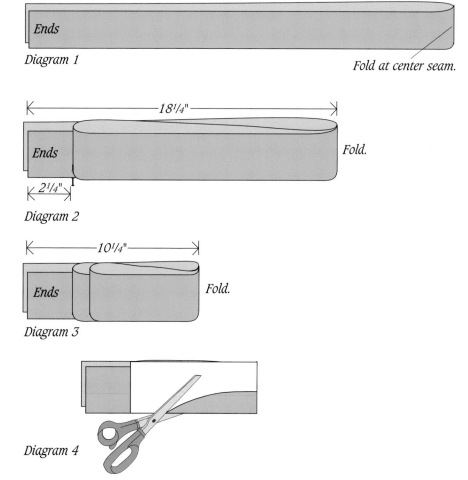

Diagram 1
34¼"
Ends
Fold at center seam.

18¼"
Ends
Fold.
2¼"
Diagram 2

10¼"
Ends
Fold.
Diagram 3

Diagram 4

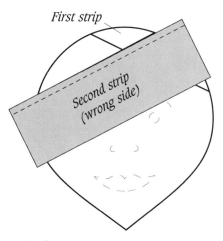

First strip
Second strip (wrong side)

Hair Placement Diagram

Quilt Top Assembly

1. Referring to photograph, join shelf rows.

2. Matching centers, sew shorter tan border strips to top and bottom edges; then sew longer strips to quilt sides.

3. Join orange border strips to make 2 (3½" x 84½") strips and 2 (3½" x 78½") strips. Join longer strips to side edges of quilt; then add shorter borders to top and bottom edges.

4. For top outer border, join 2 (7½" x 40") striped strips to make 1 (78½"-long) border. Sew border to top edge of quilt.

5. For bottom outer border, join 2 (7½" x 35") striped strips to make 1 (68½"-long) border. Sew 5½" x 7½" orange pieces to ends. Sew border to bottom edge of quilt.

6. Join 100½"-long strips to quilt sides.

Quilting and Finishing

1. Layer backing, batting, and quilt top.

2. Mark quilting lines lightly on quilt top. Quilt shown has outline quilting along arched edge of shelf top, around dolls, and around faces. Doll bodies have quilted neckties and echo quilting at ½" intervals or quilting around designs in fabric. Outer border is quilted along vertical lines of stripe print. Quilt as desired.

3. Make 290" of bias or straight-grain binding. See page 31 for directions on making and applying binding.

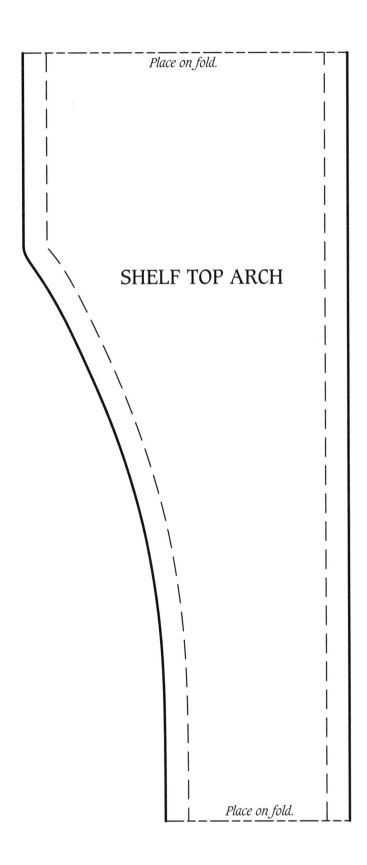

Place on fold.

SHELF TOP ARCH

Place on fold.

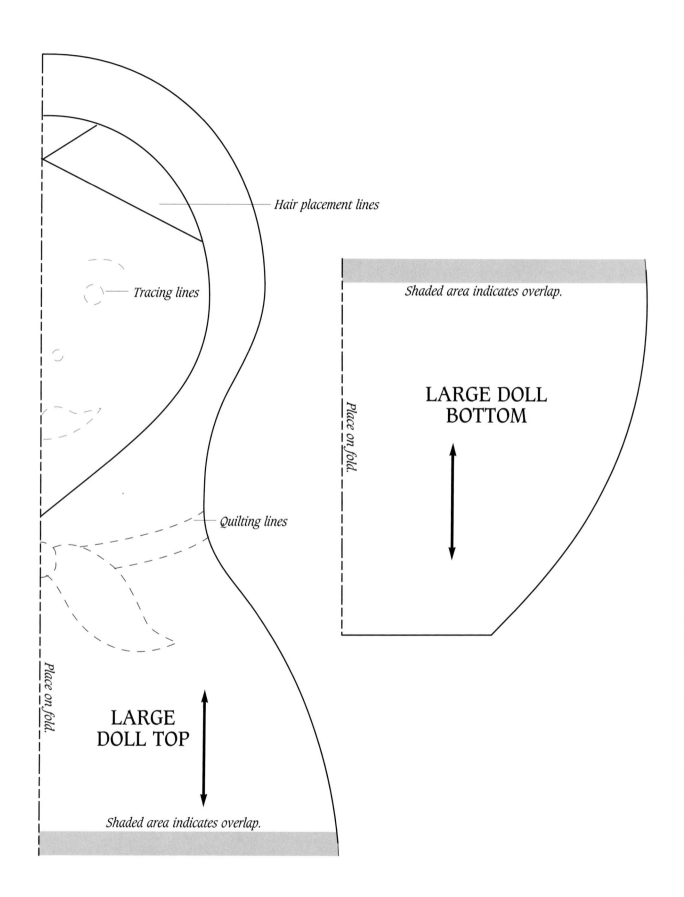

Hair placement lines

Tracing lines

Shaded area indicates overlap.

Place on fold.

LARGE DOLL
BOTTOM

Quilting lines

Place on fold.

LARGE
DOLL TOP

Shaded area indicates overlap.

132

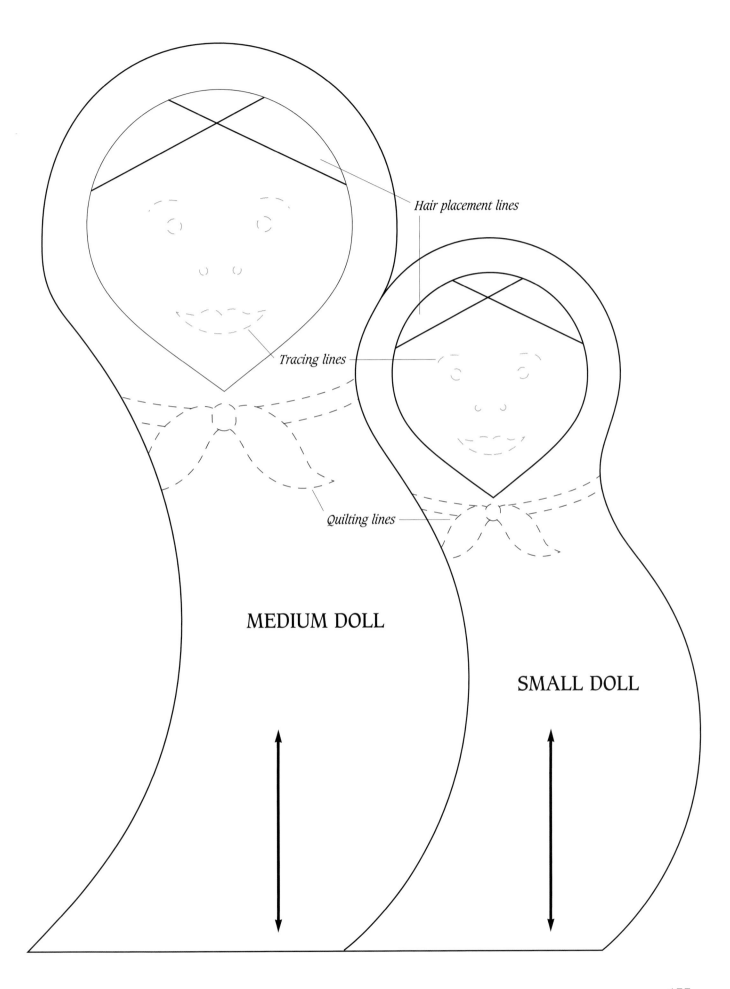

Hair placement lines

Tracing lines

Quilting lines

MEDIUM DOLL

SMALL DOLL

Ukrainian Dolls Wall Hanging

Ukrainian Dolls Wall Hanging

Three groups of dolls on a shelf make a terrific wall hanging. For a small project or a companion to the quilt, try this—it's a fun way to use up some of those exotic prints you've been saving.

Finished Size
Wall Hanging: 27" x 60"

Easy-Does-It Feature: Continuous bias

Materials
⅞ yard striped fabric for border
⅞ yard light fabric for shelf background
½ yard black plaid fabric for shelf sides
¼ yard brown plaid fabric for shelf top
⅓ yard rust-brown fabric for shelf base
3 (8" x 13") scraps for large dolls
4 (7" x 11") scraps for medium dolls
4 (5" x 9") scraps for small dolls
⅛ yard or scraps black fabric for hair
¼ yard muslin for faces
1¾ yards fabric for backing
⅝ yard fabric for binding
Black embroidery floss for facial features
Water-soluble marker
Pink permanent marker

Cutting
From **light background fabric**, cut:
  2 (15½" x 22½") pieces for shelf background.
From **black plaid fabric**, cut:
  1 (13") square for bias trim for shelf top.
  2 (4½" x 19½") pieces for shelf sides.
From **brown plaid fabric**, cut:
  2 (3½" x 26½") strips for shelf top.
From **rust-brown fabric**, cut:
  2 (4½" x 26½") pieces for shelf base.
From **striped fabric**, cut:
  2 (4½" x 27½") lengthwise strips for side borders.
  4 (4½" x 26¼") cross-grain strips for top and bottom borders.
From **black fabric**, cut:
  11 (1" x 4") strips for hair.

Making Shelf

Make template of Shelf Top Arch pattern on page 131.

1. Refer to instructions for quilt (page 129) to assemble shelf, shelf base, and sides. Wall hanging shelf is smaller. Assembled shelf unit will measure 19½" x 52½".

2. Join brown plaid strips at 1 end to make 1 (3½" x 52½") strip for shelf top.

3. With wrong sides facing, fold strip in half at center seam, matching ends. Referring to *Diagram 1,* measure 2¼" from ends and mark. Starting from marked line, measure and mark 3 (8"-long) segments along strip length, ending at center seam.

4. Fold on third marked line, bringing center fold to second marked line *(Diagram 2).* Fold again, aligning right-hand fold with first marked line *(Diagram 3).* You will have 6 layers of fabric, except at ends.

5. Lay arch template on folded strip, aligning straight edge at top and bottom of template with fabric and ends of template with folds of fabric *(Diagram 4).* Cut bottom curved edge of strip through all layers to make arches.

6. Referring to instructions on page 31, make 70" of 1"-wide continuous bias from 13" square of black plaid fabric. With wrong sides facing, fold bias in half lengthwise and press.

7. With right sides facing and raw edges aligned, pin bias strip to bottom (curved) edge of shelf top strip. Stitch through all layers, ¼" from raw edge. Turn seam allowance up and press in place so ¼" of bias trim shows beyond finished edge of arches.

8. Matching top edges and center seams, pin shelf top to shelf panel, with both pieces right side up. Topstitch in-the-ditch along bias trim seam line to join shelf top to shelf panel. Trim fabric behind shelf top, leaving ¼" seam allowance.

Appliquéing Dolls

Referring to Preparing Doll Faces and to Appliquéing Dolls sections on page 130, follow instructions to make 3 large dolls, 3 medium dolls, 1 medium doll reversed, 3 small dolls, and 1 small doll reversed. Referring to wall hanging photograph, arrange dolls in 3 groups as shown. Pin dolls on shelf and appliqué in place.

Adding Border

1. Join 2 cross-grain strips of border fabric to make 1 (55½"-long) border. Sew border to top edge of wall hanging. Press seam allowances and trim ends of border strip even with sides. Repeat for bottom border.

2. Sew lengthwise strips to sides.

Quilting and Finishing

1. Layer backing, batting, and quilt top. Quilt as desired.

2. Make 180" of bias or straight-grain binding. See page 31 for directions on making and applying binding.

3. See page 32 for directions on making a hanging sleeve.

gem from **georgia**

Since the smaller dolls nestle into either side of the large doll when reversed, play with the arrangement on each shelf before cutting the dolls from fabric.

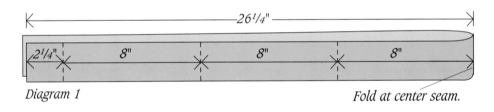

Diagram 1

Fold at center seam.

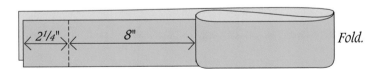

Diagram 2

Fold.

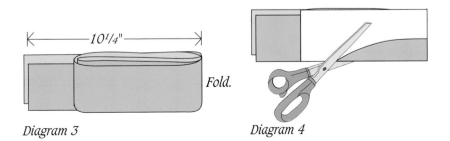

Diagram 3

Fold.

Diagram 4

Yackety Yack

136

Yackety Yack

It's a patchwork tête-à-tête as these positive and negative faces dispel the quiet with their chattering. This contemporary wall hanging gives you an opportunity for creative play with mirror-image blocks.

Finished Size
Blocks: 16 (6") blocks
Wall Hanging: 39½" x 39½"

Easy-Does-It Feature: Speed cutting with mirror-image templates

Materials
½ yard light fabric for faces
⅝ yard total assorted dark fabrics for faces and sashing squares
½ yard bright fabric for sashing
¼ yard light print for inner border
1¼ yards dark fabric for outer borders and binding
2½ yards fabric for backing
Metallic thread for quilting

Cutting
Make templates for patterns A–F on page 139.
From **assorted dark fabrics,** cut:
  8 each of A–F.
  8 each of A–F reversed.
  25 (2") sashing squares.
From **light fabric,** cut:
  8 each of A–F.
  8 each of A–F reversed.
From **bright fabric,** cut:
  40 (2" x 6½") strips for sashing.
From **light print fabric,** cut:
  4 (1½" x 34") strips for inner border.
From **dark fabric,** cut:
  4 (3½" x 40") strips for outer borders.
  20" square for bias binding.

Piecing Blocks
1. Following *Block 1 Assembly Diagram,* join pieces A–F to make light face; then join remaining pieces A–F to make dark face. Join faces to make block. Repeat to make 8 Block 1s.
2. Follow *Block 2 Assembly Diagram* to make 8 Block 2s in same manner.

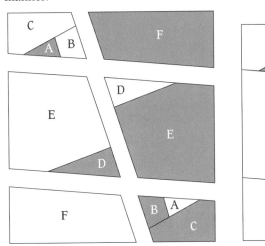

Block 1 Assembly Diagram—Make 8.

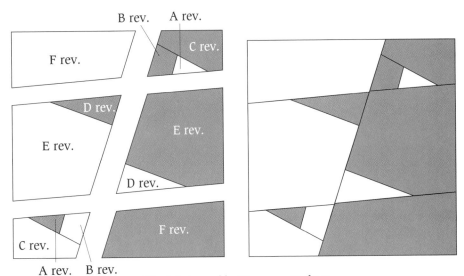

Block 2 Assembly Diagram—Make 8.

gem from georgia

To cut out mirror-image pieces easily, stack the light and dark fabrics with right sides facing. Then cut out both images at one time.

Quilt Top Assembly

1. Referring to *Quilt Top Assembly Diagram,* join 4 Block 1s and 5 sashing strips to make 1 horizontal row as shown. Repeat to make a second Block 1 row. In same manner, make 2 Block 2 rows.

2. Join 5 sashing squares and 4 sashing strips to make 1 horizontal sashing row. Repeat to make 5 rows.

3. Join sashing rows and block rows as shown.

4. Join 1½" x 34" light print strips to quilt, mitering corners.

5. Join 3½" x 40" dark strips to quilt, mitering corners.

Quilting and Finishing

1. Layer backing, batting, and quilt top. Baste.

2. Outline-quilt each face by hand. Machine-quilt a zigzag design through sashing with metallic thread.

3. If you have a computerized sewing machine, program it to spell "Yackety Yack" in outer border if desired. Or choose a simple straight or zigzag pattern.

4. Make 135" of bias or straight-grain binding from 20" square. See page 31 for directions on making and applying binding.

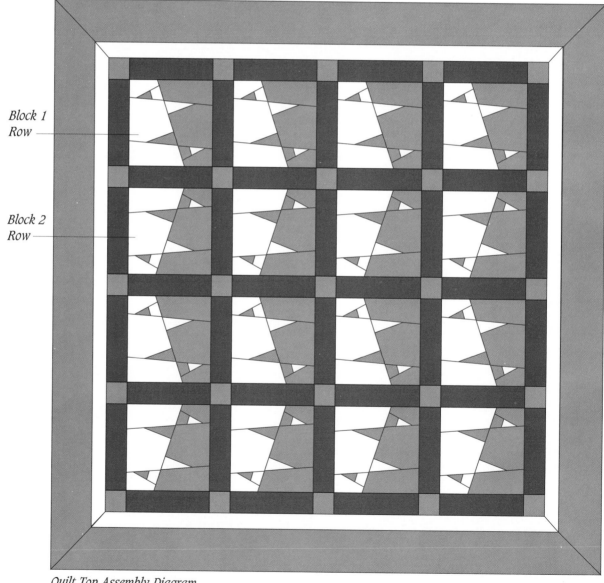

Block 1 Row

Block 2 Row

Quilt Top Assembly Diagram

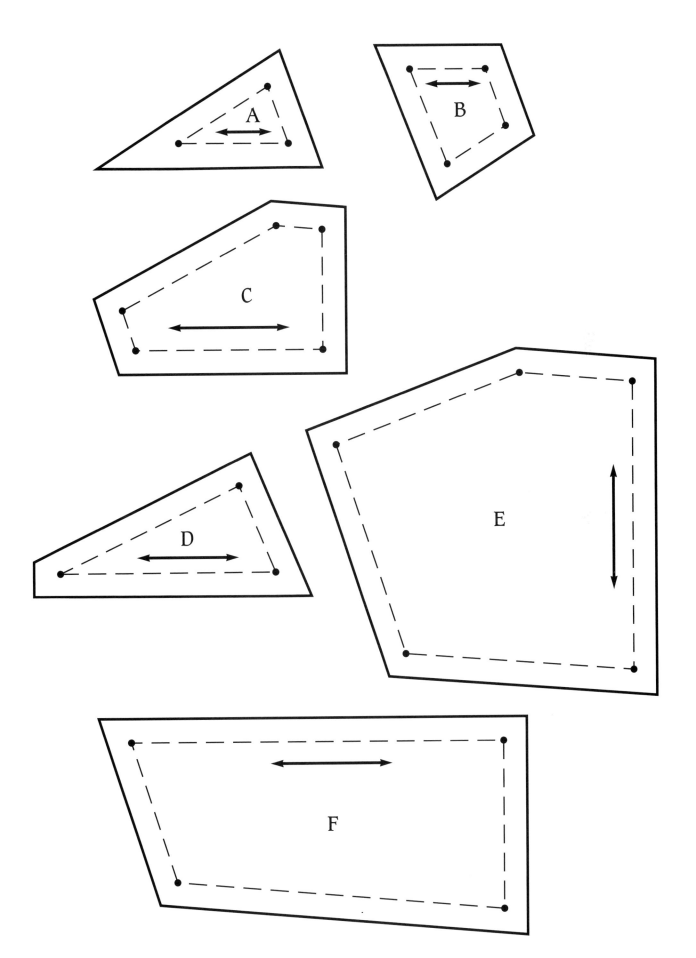

Tartan Thistle

Tartan Thistle

A variety of plaids enhances the distinctive silhouette of the thistle in this striking quilt. Machine reverse appliqué and red quilting thread emphasize its dramatic simplicity.

Finished Size
Blocks: 18 (16") reverse-appliqué blocks
Quilt: 79" x 105"

Easy-Does-It Feature: Machine reverse appliqué

Materials
5⅝ yards black for backgrounds and binding
1 (15" x 19") rectangle each of 18 assorted plaids for thistles and sashing squares
2⅛ yards plaid for side triangles
1½ yards red print for sashing
3 yards 108"-wide fabric for backing or 6 yards 45"-wide fabric
Freezer paper
Tear-away stabilizer
Red quilting thread

Cutting
Using pieces A, B, and C on pages 143–145, make pattern for complete thistle by tracing pattern onto freezer paper. Cut out.
From **black fabric,** cut:
  18 (16½") background squares.
  1 (33") square for binding.
From **2⅛ yards of plaid,** cut:
  3 (27") squares. Cut each in quarters diagonally to make 12 side triangles (you will have 2 left over).
  2 (15") squares. Cut each in half diagonally to make 4 corner triangles.
From **red print,** cut:
  48 (2½" x 16½") strips for sashing.
From **freezer paper,** cut:
  6 thistle templates, using pattern. (Each freezer-paper template can be used at least 3 times.)

Piecing Blocks
1. To cut thistle, iron shiny side of 1 freezer-paper template to wrong side of 1 (15" x 19") plaid rectangle.
2. Cut out thistle, adding ½" seam allowance, except at bottom point of stem *(Diagram 1)*.
3. To appliqué block, fold 1 black 16½" square in half diagonally and crease to make placement guide.
4. With right side of plaid facing wrong side of block, center thistle along crease of black square, with point of stem aligned with corner of square. Pin or baste in place.
5. Using a straightstitch, stitch plaid thistle to background square along edge of paper template. Begin and end at stem to eliminate wrinkles *(Diagram 2)*. Remove template.
6. Turn block right side up. Using appliqué scissors, carefully cut away black fabric inside sewing lines in 1 complete piece to reveal plaid fabric underneath *(Diagram 3)*. Save black cutout for side triangles.
7. Lay tear-away stabilizer under block. With a narrow satin stitch, machine-stitch around all edges of thistle.
8. Trim away any excess plaid fabric from back.
9. Repeat steps 1–8 to make 18 blocks.

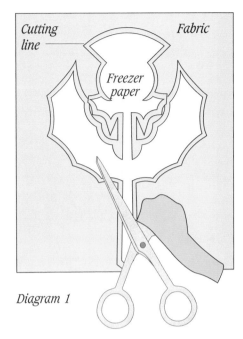

Diagram 1

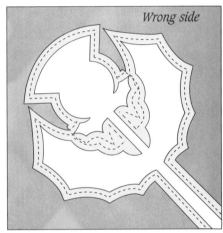

Diagram 2

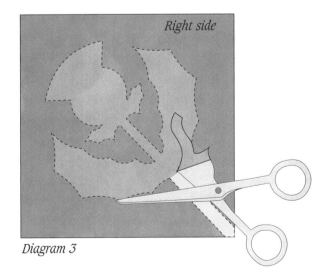

Diagram 3

10. Spray black thistle cutouts with spray sizing to add stability. Lay cutouts on right side of plaid setting triangles as shown in *Quilt Top Assembly Diagram.* Baste.

11. Machine-appliqué cutouts in place with a narrow satin stitch. Trim excess.

12. From plaid scraps, cut 31 (2½") sashing squares.

Quilt Top Assembly

1. Referring to *Quilt Top Assembly Diagram,* arrange all pieces in diagonal rows as shown.

2. Join blocks, sashing, and sashing squares in each row. Add side and corner triangles to ends of rows.

3. Join rows.

Quilting and Finishing

1. Layer backing, batting, and quilt top. Baste.

2. Using red quilting thread, outline-quilt each block and each thistle. Add echo quilting, if desired.

3. Make 410" of bias binding from 33" square. See page 31 for directions on making and applying binding.

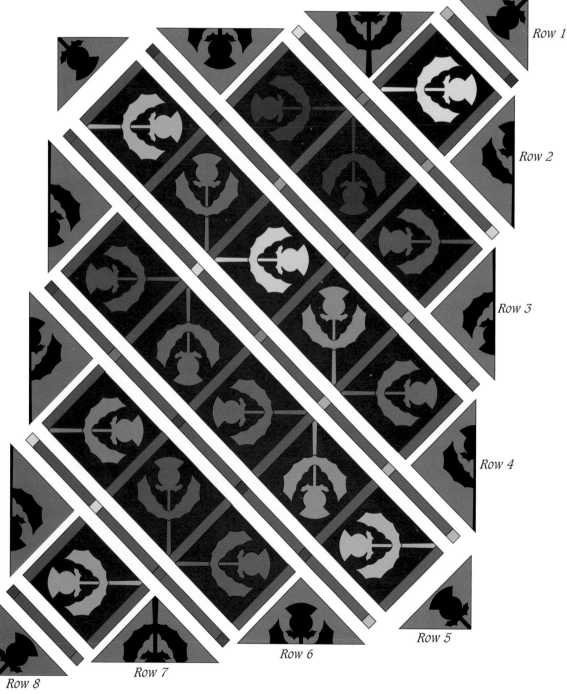

Row 1

Row 2

Row 3

Row 4

Row 5

Row 6

Row 7

Row 8

Quilt Top Assembly Diagram

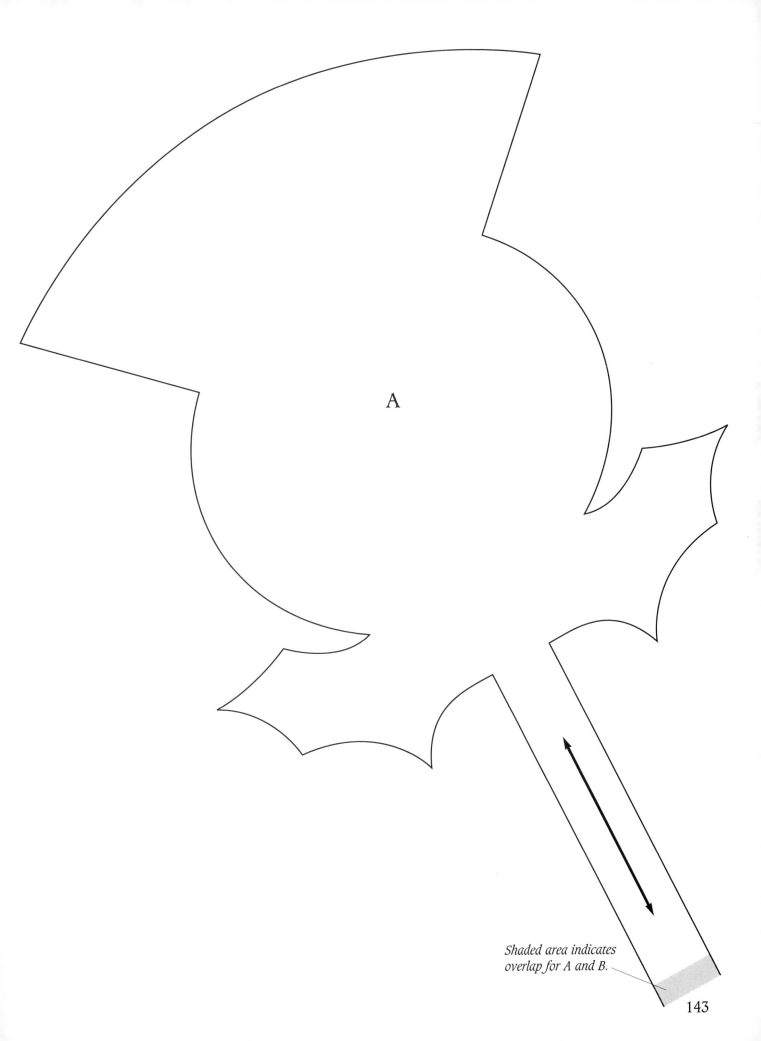

A

Shaded area indicates overlap for A and B.

143

A

C   C rev.

B

*After you transfer
all pattern pieces
onto freezer paper,
your complete Thistle
Pattern will look like
this.*

*Placement Diagram for
Complete Thistle Pattern*

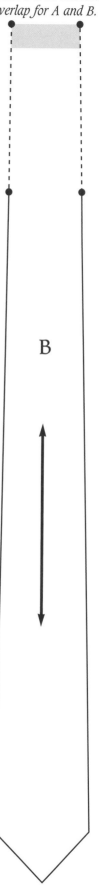

*Shaded area indicates
overlap for A and B.*

B

**gem
from
georgia**

*When using dark fabrics for a quilt, use
dark gray batting so that small fibers that
might beard through will be less visible.*

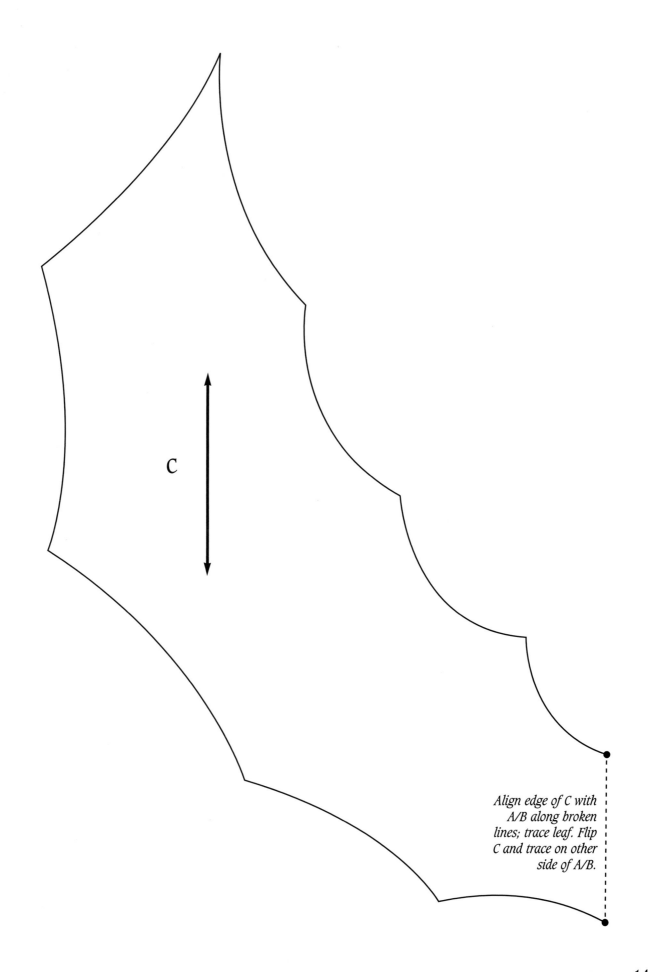

C

Align edge of C with A/B along broken lines; trace leaf. Flip C and trace on other side of A/B.

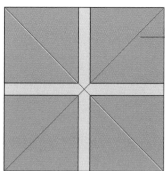

Diagram 1

Appliqué placement lines

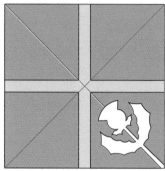

Diagram 2

Thistle Table Topper

Brighten your kitchen or a friend's with a thistle table topper. You can make this project in one evening to add instant color to your room. Best of all, the more it's washed, the better it frays!

Finished Size
Table Topper: 34" square

Materials
34" square bright fabric
4 (16") squares contrasting woven plaid
Freezer paper

Directions
1. Using pieces A, B, and C on pages 143–145, make pattern for complete thistle by tracing pattern onto freezer paper. Cut out.

2. To make placement lines, press each 16" square in half diagonally. Press 34" square in quarters diagonally.

3. Lay 16" squares right side up on corners of 34" square, aligning diagonal lines and raw edges *(Diagram 1)*. Pin or baste in place.

4. Lay freezer-paper thistle pattern on 1 (16") square along diagonal line, with point of stem in corner *(Diagram 2)*. Press in place.

5. Stitch around thistle, using edge of template as a guide *(Diagram 3)*.

6. Remove template. Using appliqué scissors, carefully cut away plaid fabric ¼" inside sewing lines to reveal fabric underneath *(Diagram 4)*. Repeat for each block.

7. Using a short stitch length, stitch around all edges of plaid squares, ¼" from edge.

8. Fray edges of thistles and all edges of cloth backing to stitching line.

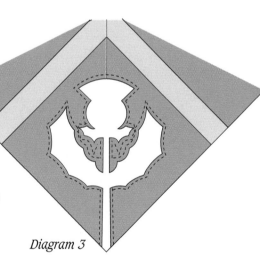

Diagram 3

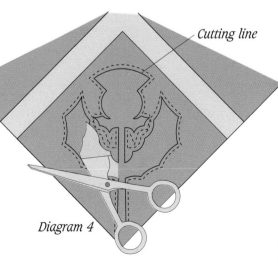

Cutting line

Diagram 4

Tartan Thistle Vest

This quick, reversible vest is a great way to dress up a T-shirt and a pair of jeans.

Materials
Vest pattern of your choice
3 reversible woven plaids in contrasting colors (enough to make a vest from each one)
Freezer paper

Directions
1. Cut out pieces of vest in all 3 colors.

2. Sew shoulder and side seams of each set.

3. Decide which plaid will be outer, middle, and inner layers of vest. Stack inner layer (right side down), middle layer (right side up), and outer layer (right side up). Baste.

4. Using pieces A, B, and C on pages 143–145, make pattern for complete thistle by tracing pattern onto freezer paper. Cut out.

5. Center freezer-paper thistle on outer layer of vest back. Press in place.

6. Stitch around thistle, using edges of template as a guide *(Diagram 1)*.

7. Remove template.

8. Cut away outer layer of vest ¼" inside sewing lines to reveal middle layer of vest *(Diagram 2)*. Repeat to cut away inner layer of vest.

9. Cut template in half vertically.

10. Center each half on outer layer of vest front (see photo). Stitch and cut in same manner as for back.

11. Topstitch ¼" from raw edges around outer edges of vest and armholes through all layers. Repeat topstitching to strengthen seams.

12. Fray thistles and raw edges.

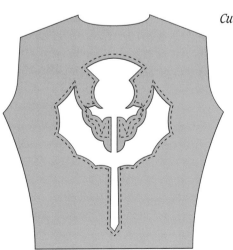

Diagram 1

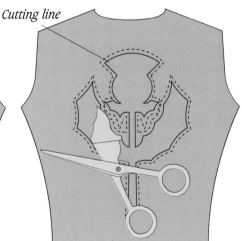

Cutting line

Diagram 2

Quilting Around the World

Quilting Around the World

I chose 36 bright fabrics in a world of colors for this globe. The gentle curves are easy to stitch either by hand or by machine.

Finished Size
Quilt: 20" x 20"

Easy-Does-It Feature: Easy curves

Materials
36 (6"-square) assorted scrap fabrics
¼ yard white-on-white fabric for background
⅛ yard black fabric for inner border
⅝ yard striped fabric for outer border and binding
22" square for backing

Cutting
Make templates for patterns A–J on pages 150 and 151.
From **scrap fabrics,** cut:
  2 each of A–I. Flip templates over and cut 2 reverse of each.
From **white-on-white fabric,** cut:
  4 Js.
From **black fabric,** cut:
  2 (1½" x 14½") strips for inner border.
  2 (1½" x 16½") strips for inner border.
From **striped fabric,** cut:
  4 (2½" x 20½") strips for outer border.
  15" square for bias binding.

Piecing Blocks
1. Referring to *Diagram 1*, join A, B, and C to make Unit 1.
2. Join D, E, and F to make Unit 2.
3. Join G, H, and I to make Unit 3.
4. Join units. Add J to outside edge to complete quarter.
5. Repeat with reversed pieces to make second quarter *(Diagram 2).* Join quarters for top half of globe.
6. Repeat steps 1–5 to make bottom half of globe.
7. Join halves.

Quilt Top Assembly
1. Join 1½" x 14½" black strips to top and bottom of quilt.
2. Join 1½" x 16½" black strips to sides of quilt.
3. Join 4 (2½" x 20½") striped strips to quilt, mitering corners.

Quilting and Finishing
1. Layer backing, batting, and quilt top. Baste.
2. Quilt gently curving longitude and latitude lines through globe.
3. Outline-quilt Js and borders.
4. Make 80" bias or straight-grain binding from 15" square. See page 31 for directions on making and applying binding.

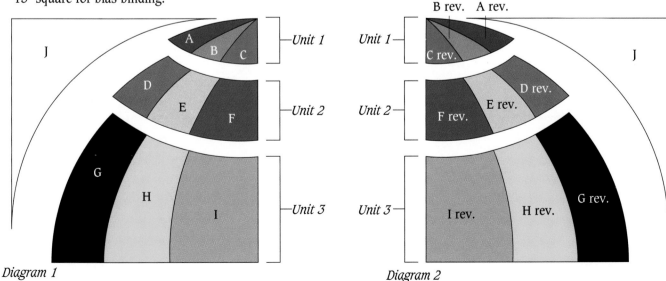

Diagram 1

Diagram 2

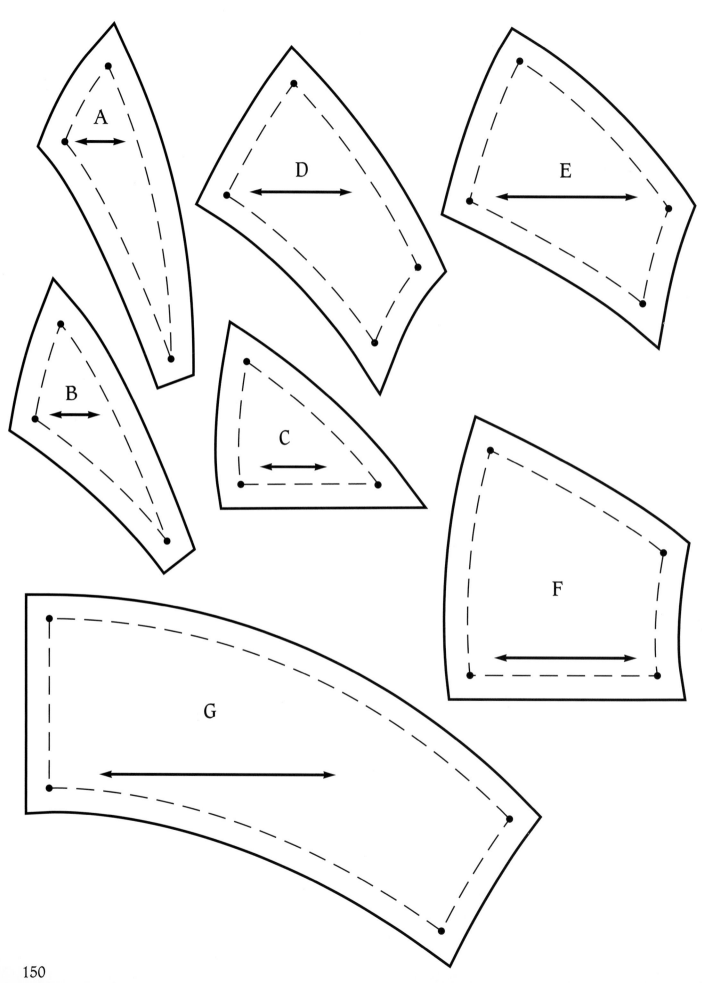

A

D

E

B

C

F

G

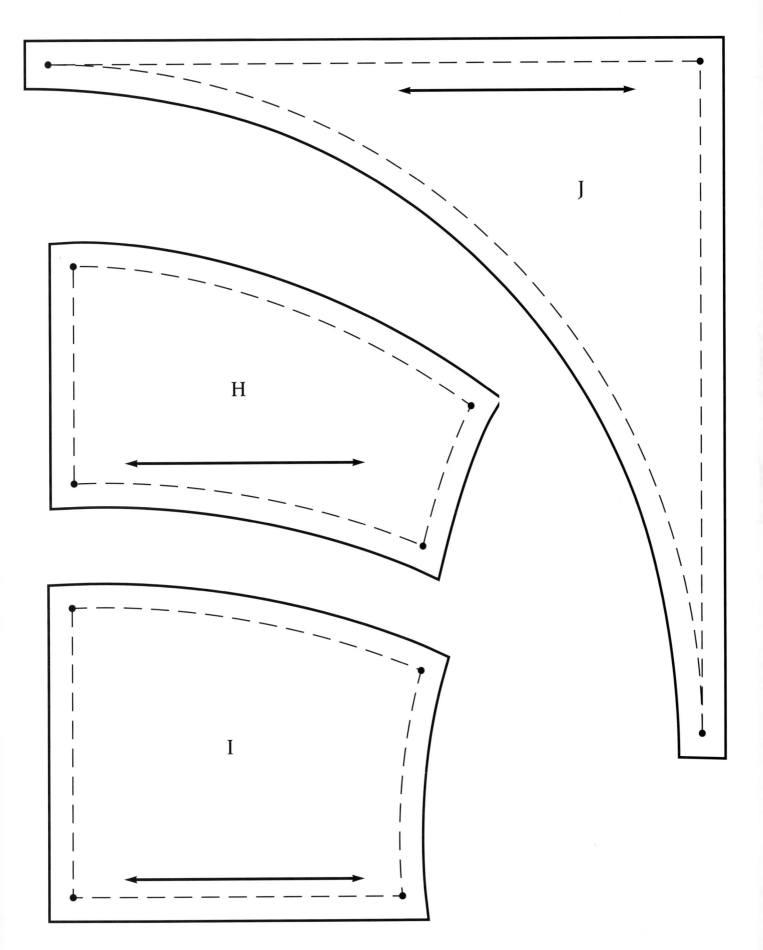

J

H

I

151

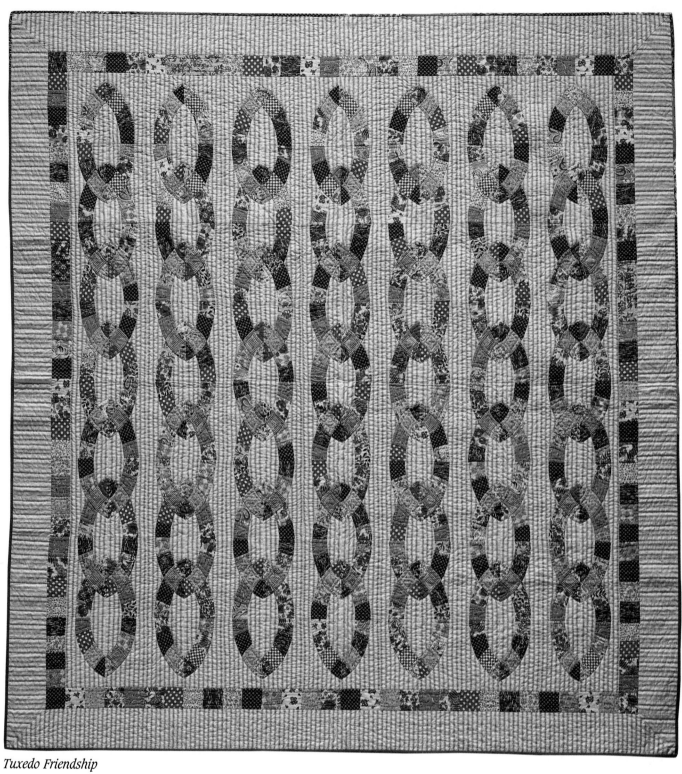

Tuxedo Friendship

Tuxedo Friendship

Oval links reminiscent of the Double Wedding Ring intertwine down the length of this colorful quilt. Set against a field of blue-and-white ticking, the feedsack pieces add old-time flair. The quilt's name comes from the Tuxedo Feed Sack Company, whose name is stamped on one of the fabrics.

Finished Size

Blocks: 42 (10") blocks and 14 (8½" x 10") blocks
Quilt: 85" x 92"

Easy-Does-It Feature: Simplified piecing to avoid set-in seams

Materials

4¾ yards total of assorted print scraps
5½ yards striped background fabric
2½ yards 108"-wide backing fabric or 5½ yards 45"-wide fabric
32½" square or 1 yard fabric for bias binding*
*Note: The quiltmaker combined solid and print bias strips to make the binding on this quilt.

Cutting

Make templates for patterns A–H on pages 156 and 157.
From **assorted print scraps,** cut:
  98 pieces each of A, A rev., B, B rev., D, and D rev.
  112 Cs.
  128 (3") squares for inner border.
From **striped fabric,** cut:
  9 (5½"-wide) crosswise strips for outer borders.
  84 pieces each of E, E rev., and F.
  14 pieces each of G, G rev., H, and H rev.

Piecing Block 1

1. To make right half of block, join 1 A to 1 B *(Diagram 1)*. Join A/B unit to 1 E *(Diagram 2)*. Join 1 F to A/B/E unit *(Diagram 3)*. Press seams toward E.

2. Join 1 A rev., 1 B rev., 1 C, and 1 D *(Diagram 4)*. Join 1 E rev. to 1 D rev. *(Diagram 5)*. Join these 2 units *(Diagram 6)*.

Diagram 1

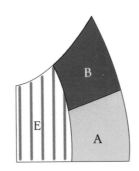

Diagram 2

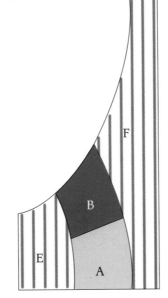

Diagram 3

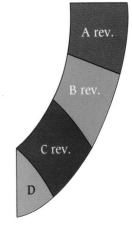

Diagram 4

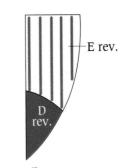

Diagram 5

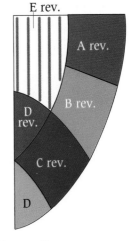

Diagram 6

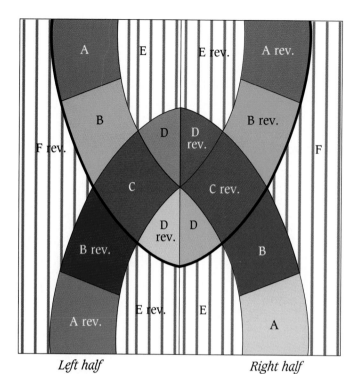

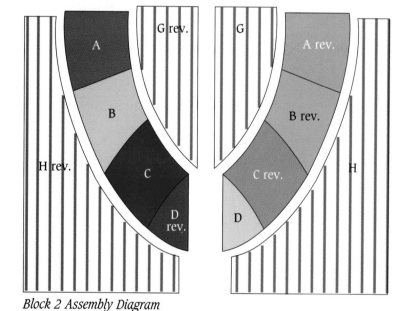

Block 1 Assembly Diagram

Left half   *Right half*

Block 2 Assembly Diagram

3. Join pieced unit to A/B/E/F unit to complete right half of block *(Block 1 Assembly Diagram)*. *Note:* Heavy black line on diagram indicates seam line between units. Make left half of block in same manner as shown.

4. Join halves as shown to make block.

5. Repeat to make 42 Block 1s.

Piecing Block 2
Follow *Block 2 Assembly Diagram* to make 14 Block 2s.

Quilt Top Assembly
1. Referring to *Quilt Top Assembly Diagram,* join 6 Block 1s vertically. Add a Block 2 to top and bottom of each row. Repeat to make 7 vertical rows.

2. Join rows.

3. Join 34 (3") squares each to make 2 (85"-long) strips for side borders. Join 29 (3") squares each to make 2 (72½"-long) strips for top and bottom borders. Add borders to quilt, trimming any excess.

4. From 5½"-wide crosswise strips of striped fabric, make 2 (85½"-long) strips for top and bottom borders and 2 (92½"-long) strips for each side border.

5. Join borders to quilt, mitering corners.

Quilting and Finishing
1. Layer backing, batting, and quilt top. Baste.

2. Quilt straight lines along stripes on fabric. Outline-quilt ½" inside each scrap fabric.

3. Make 405" of bias binding from 32½" square or from bias strips of assorted fabrics. See page 31 for directions on making and applying binding.

gem from georgia

As you can see from this quilt, not all feed sacks were plain white. Search your antiques shops, exchange with friends, or even join a Feed Sack Club to acquire a medley of old fabrics.

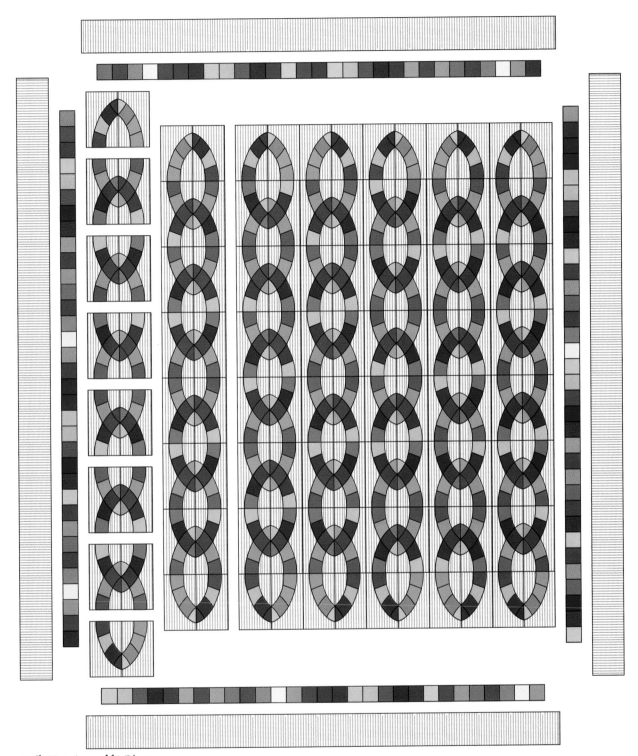

Quilt Top Assembly Diagram

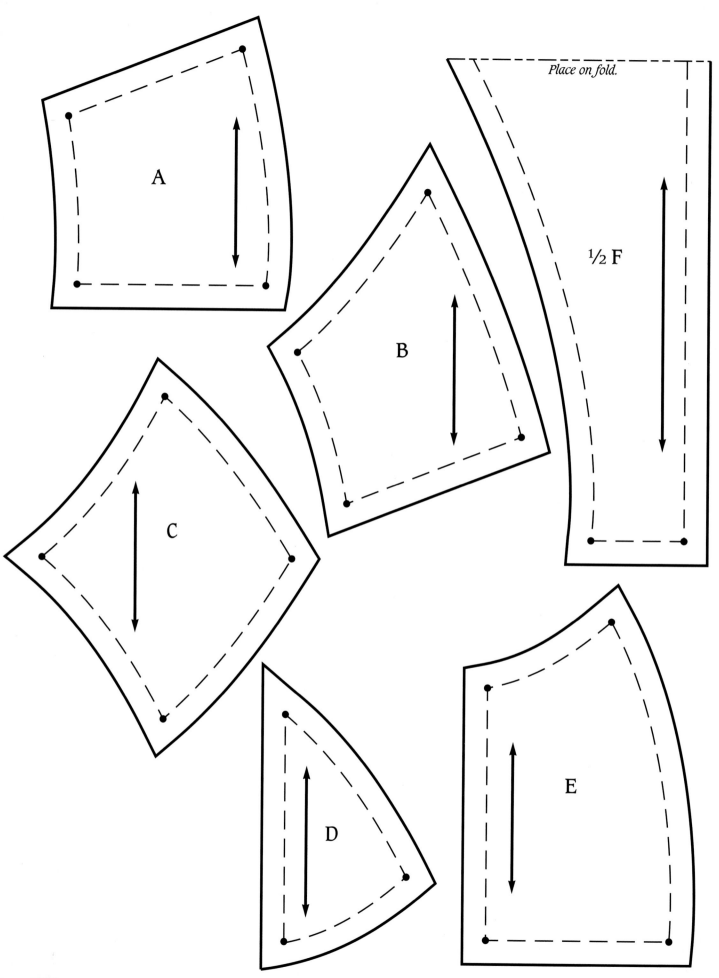

A

B

Place on fold.

½ F

C

D

E

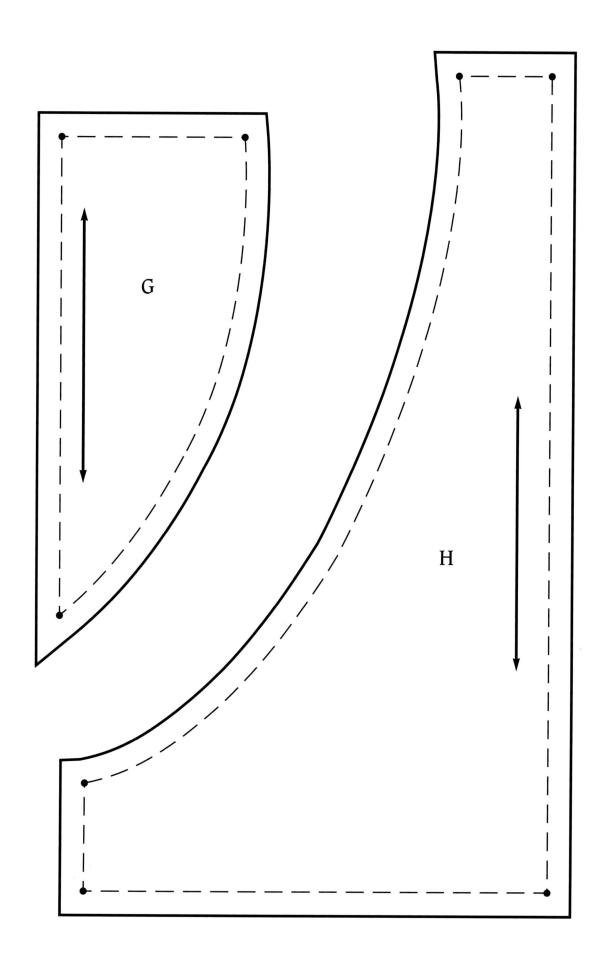

G

H

157

Georgia's Gallery

Some people take photographs to remember important events—I make quilts! Let me share a few of my favorites here. Then feel free to experiment as you create your own fabric memories.

DUTCH TREAT
Made by Georgia J. Bonesteel as a tribute to new-found Dutch friends.

BIG SKY COUNTRY
*Made by Georgia J. Bonesteel;
inspired by a mountain view
from a Western ranch.*

SUNRISE, SUN-TIES
*Made by Georgia J. Bonesteel;
inspired by a design on an
iron fence.*

Designs continued on next page.

BONNIE BLUE RIDGE

*Made by Georgia J. Bonesteel
for the Southeastern Chapter
of the American
Rhododendron Society.*

TREE OF LIFE

*Made by Georgia J. Bonesteel
for daughter Amy upon her
marriage.*